The Art of War: Famous Military Strategies from History

Anam Rasheed

Published by Anam Rasheed, 2024.

While every precaution has been taken in the preparation of this book, the publisher assumes no responsibility for errors or omissions, or for damages resulting from the use of the information contained herein.

THE ART OF WAR: FAMOUS MILITARY STRATEGIES FROM HISTORY

First edition. November 8, 2024.

Copyright © 2024 Anam Rasheed.

ISBN: 979-8227011718

Written by Anam Rasheed.

Table of Contents

Prologue 1
Chapter 1: The Power of Surprise 2
Chapter 2: Ancient Ambush Tactics 5
Chapter 3: Defending the High Ground 9
Chapter 4: The Use of Camouflage 13
Chapter 5: The Importance of Spies 18
Chapter 6: Fortresses and Strongholds 23
Chapter 7: Lightning Speed Attacks 28
Chapter 8: The Art of Retreating 33
Chapter 9: Deception on the Battlefield 39
Chapter 10: Guerrilla Warfare Secrets 44
Chapter 11: The Power of Alliances 50
Chapter 12: Siege Warfare Techniques 55
Chapter 13: Night Raids and Stealth Moves 61
Chapter 14: Sea Battles and Naval Strategy 66
Chapter 15: The Role of Psychological Warfare 71
Chapter 16: Using Nature as an Ally 76
Chapter 17: Heroic Last Stands 82
Chapter 18: Technology in Battle 87
Chapter 19: Communication on the Battlefield 93
Chapter 20: Courage and Leadership 99
Epilogue 105

Prologue

Throughout history, battles have been fought for freedom, power, resources, and survival. Behind each battle, there was more than just courage and strength; there was strategy—the clever planning that helped armies outsmart their opponents. Military leaders have always known that wars are not just won with weapons; they're also won with wisdom, patience, and sometimes even trickery. In every time period and every part of the world, great minds have created strategies to change the course of history.

This book will take you on a journey through some of the most fascinating military strategies ever used. From ancient ambushes in forests to clever escapes across mountains, from defending castle walls to navigating vast seas, you'll discover the incredible tactics that shaped battles and entire nations. You'll learn how armies and leaders used everything they had—the land, their knowledge of the enemy, and even the stars at night—to gain the upper hand.

Each chapter will explore a different type of strategy, giving you a peek into the minds of historical leaders and showing you the skills that made their plans so successful. You'll see how clever thinking can make all the difference and how a single smart decision can turn the tide of war.

Are you ready to step into the world of ancient generals, fierce warriors, and brilliant strategists? Turn the page, and let's discover the art of war together.

Chapter 1: The Power of Surprise

Imagine you're playing a game with friends where the goal is to tag each other. Now, if you run straight at them, they'll probably see you coming and move out of the way. But, if you quietly come up from behind or surprise them by popping out from a hiding spot, they're less likely to escape! This idea of catching someone off guard is one of the oldest and most powerful strategies in history. In battles, just like in games, surprising the other side can make a huge difference, and many armies have used the power of surprise to win even when they had fewer soldiers or less powerful weapons.

In history, some of the best-known leaders and generals used surprise to their advantage. Imagine being a soldier in an ancient army. You're marching along a mountain trail, feeling pretty safe because you're far from the enemy. Suddenly, they appear from above, launching an attack! This was a trick used by armies like the Roman army or Mongol warriors, who often attacked when the enemy was least expecting it. Sometimes, soldiers would even come out of forests, hillsides, or rivers, places that seemed safe or empty, catching the enemy completely unprepared. In fact, armies might attack at night or during terrible weather, times when no one expected a fight. By doing this, they didn't give the enemy time to get organized or set up defenses.

One of the most famous stories of surprise in war is the Greek story of the Trojan Horse. Thousands of years ago, the Greeks were in a long war with the Trojans. The Greeks came up with a clever trick to get inside the heavily protected city of Troy. They built a huge wooden horse and hid some of their soldiers inside it, then pretended to give up on the battle and sailed away. The Trojans thought the horse was a gift, and they brought it into their city as a trophy. But that night, Greek soldiers crept out of the horse and opened the city gates, allowing the rest of the Greek army to sneak in and capture Troy. This trick is still remembered today as one of the greatest surprises in history!

Another great example comes from World War II, which took place not that long ago. There was a famous attack called the "D-Day" invasion, where thousands of soldiers landed on the beaches of France to surprise the enemy. The leaders of this attack did everything they could to keep it a secret. They tricked the enemy by setting up fake tanks and equipment in a different area, making them think the attack would happen somewhere else. Then, when the real attack happened, the enemy was so shocked that they weren't ready in time to stop it. By surprising their opponents, these soldiers gained a huge advantage.

Surprises don't just happen on land. There have also been surprise attacks on the water! In the 16th century, there was a famous English sea captain named Sir Francis Drake who was known for his surprise attacks against Spanish ships. He would sneak up on them using fog or the cover of night, striking when they were least expecting it. With these surprise attacks, he was able to win battles and even capture treasure despite not having the biggest or most powerful fleet.

Surprise was also used by smaller armies fighting for their freedom. During the American Revolution, American soldiers used surprise attacks, which they called "guerrilla warfare." They didn't have the huge, organized army that the British did, so they came up with ways to strike quickly and then vanish. They would hide in forests, wait for British troops to pass by, then rush out, attack, and quickly retreat before the British could fight back. This way, they could weaken a much stronger enemy little by little.

But surprise isn't just about sneaking up quietly. It can also mean surprising the enemy with unusual tactics. For instance, Hannibal, a general from ancient Carthage, surprised the Roman army by leading his soldiers and even war elephants over the snowy Alps mountains to attack Rome from a direction no one thought possible. The Romans expected him to come from the south, but Hannibal took a different route that was very difficult, catching the Romans off guard. Imagine their shock when they saw huge elephants in places they never expected!

Surprises in war often work because they create confusion and panic. When soldiers don't know what's happening or are caught off guard, they don't have time to prepare and can make mistakes. This gives the other side a chance to gain control. For example, in the Battle of Trenton during the American Revolution, General George Washington led his troops across the icy Delaware River on Christmas night. The enemy soldiers, called Hessians, were celebrating the holiday and didn't expect a fight. Washington's army surprised them and won a quick victory, boosting the morale of his troops and inspiring others to join their fight.

The power of surprise is all about doing the unexpected. In many cases, surprise can make an army feel like they're everywhere at once, even when they have fewer people. It's like playing a tricky game of hide-and-seek with strategy, where you use timing, careful planning, and clever ideas to outsmart your opponent. The most successful surprise attacks have shaped history and show that clever thinking and timing can sometimes be more important than strength alone.

Chapter 2: Ancient Ambush Tactics

In ancient times, when armies didn't have high-tech weapons or advanced communication, they had to rely on clever tricks to win battles. One of the most powerful tactics was the ambush. An ambush is a surprise attack that's carefully planned to catch the enemy off guard. Picture walking through a forest, thinking you're safe, and suddenly soldiers jump out from behind trees and bushes! Armies used ambushes to shock their enemies, using the element of surprise to turn the tide of battles, especially if they were outnumbered or less equipped. This tactic was popular all over the world, from Asia to Europe, and each culture had its own way of making ambushes work.

One of the most famous examples of an ambush in history was the Battle of the Teutoburg Forest. This happened over 2,000 years ago when the Roman Empire, one of the biggest and most powerful empires at the time, tried to expand into lands in modern-day Germany. The Romans were confident as they marched through the dense, dark forest, not expecting trouble. But Arminius, a Germanic leader, had a plan. He knew the Romans' path through the forest, so he gathered his warriors and hid them along the narrow trail. The Romans, weighed down by heavy armor and supplies, didn't see the attack coming. The ambush worked because the Germans knew the terrain well, while the Romans were lost and surrounded by trees, making it hard to defend themselves. In the end, Arminius's warriors defeated the Roman legions, which shocked the Roman Empire and stopped their plans to conquer the area. This ambush changed history by keeping the Roman Empire from spreading further into Germanic lands.

Ambushes often involved trickery, like pretending to retreat to lure the enemy into a trap. In ancient China, famous generals would often pretend to flee, leaving behind what seemed like an easy path to chase them. Sun Tzu, the famous Chinese military strategist who wrote *The*

Art of War, believed ambushes were crucial for winning battles. His book teaches that "all warfare is based on deception," meaning that if you can trick your enemy, you're already halfway to victory. Many generals followed this advice. For instance, they might leave a small, weak-looking group of soldiers out in the open as bait. When the enemy took the bait and charged in, thinking they'd win easily, they'd be surrounded by hidden troops lying in wait, often concealed in forests, hillsides, or tall grass. This tactic allowed even smaller forces to overpower larger ones by catching them completely off guard.

In ancient Greece, ambushes were also a common tactic, especially among the Spartans, who were known for their strict and disciplined military lifestyle. The Spartans often used ambushes during their many wars with neighboring cities. They trained their soldiers to move quietly and quickly, teaching them to blend into the natural landscape and hide until the perfect moment. In battles, they would take advantage of hills, valleys, and riverbanks to set up traps. For example, they might wait at the top of a narrow pass and, when the enemy tried to come through, rain down arrows and stones from above. Ambushes allowed them to defeat even larger armies that tried to enter their territory, showing that a well-planned ambush could turn the tide of a battle.

Even ancient cultures like the Celts, who lived in parts of Europe like present-day Ireland and Scotland, relied heavily on ambushes. The Celts didn't have the same formal training or armor as the Roman soldiers they fought against, so they used their knowledge of the land to plan attacks from forests, hills, and rivers. Celtic warriors would hide along narrow paths, watching and waiting until they saw the enemy. Once the enemy was in the middle of the ambush site, Celtic warriors would spring out, attacking from all sides with speed and fierce battle cries. The surprise often terrified the opposing soldiers, who didn't expect an attack and struggled to fight back in the unfamiliar terrain.

This is another example of how knowing the land well gave a huge advantage to the side setting up the ambush.

One of the most famous ambush tactics was used by Hannibal, the brilliant Carthaginian general, during the Second Punic War against Rome. At the Battle of Lake Trasimene in Italy, Hannibal led his army in a way that forced the Roman soldiers to follow him along a narrow path by the lake. As the Romans marched in a long line by the water's edge, Hannibal's troops, who were hidden on the hills above, attacked. The Romans were trapped between the lake and Hannibal's soldiers, with nowhere to go. The Carthaginian soldiers rushed down the hills, and the Roman army was completely overwhelmed. This ambush was so well-executed that the Romans didn't stand a chance, and it's still remembered as one of the most successful ambushes in military history.

Ancient people also used natural features, like rivers and cliffs, to help with their ambushes. In many cases, they would wait until their enemies were crossing a river or climbing a steep hill. Since the soldiers would be busy crossing or climbing, they would be less prepared to defend themselves. For example, ancient armies in places like Japan used mountain paths to their advantage. Samurai warriors were known for planning ambushes on narrow trails through the mountains. They would hide along these trails and wait for enemy soldiers to march through. When the enemies were in a difficult spot where they couldn't spread out or defend themselves well, the samurai would strike, winning battles by taking advantage of the challenging terrain.

Ambushes were also used in ancient India, where rulers often faced invaders. In many cases, Indian armies hid in the thick jungles, using their knowledge of the environment to surprise enemies who were unfamiliar with the area. These ambushes would sometimes involve using elephants and other animals to scare the enemy, adding to the shock and confusion. In areas with rivers and swamps, ambushes could trap armies in mud, slowing them down and making them easier to defeat.

Ambush tactics were not just about fighting but also about being creative and using nature to gain an advantage. Warriors had to be patient, waiting quietly until the enemy walked into the trap. They also needed courage to stay hidden even when the enemy was close. An ambush could take hours or even days to plan and execute perfectly, requiring teamwork and trust among soldiers. Because of these skills, ambushes became an essential part of ancient warfare. They allowed smaller, less powerful groups to defend their lands and surprise larger, more powerful armies, changing the course of many battles throughout history.

Chapter 3: Defending the High Ground

Imagine you're playing a game of tag on a playground with hills. If you stand at the top of a hill, you can see everyone around you, making it harder for them to catch you. Plus, if someone tries to climb up to reach you, you can run down or even tag them easily while they struggle to come up. This idea of having an advantage by being on higher ground has been used in battles for thousands of years. Ancient armies knew that defending the high ground could give them a huge advantage in battle, and this strategy has been used in every corner of the world. High ground isn't just any tall spot; it's usually a hill, mountain, or any elevated position where soldiers can see the battlefield below and protect their position more easily.

One of the main reasons high ground is so useful in battle is because it's tough for the enemy to reach you. Imagine trying to climb a steep hill or mountain in full armor, carrying a heavy sword, shield, or other gear. Climbing alone is exhausting, but when you're trying to reach soldiers who are ready to attack from above, it becomes much harder. Defending soldiers can throw rocks, launch arrows, or roll heavy objects like logs down on the attackers as they struggle uphill. This makes it very difficult for an attacking army to keep its formation, stay organized, or defend itself. Defenders on high ground can wear down their attackers before they even reach the top, making the battle easier for those at the top.

A famous example of defending high ground happened thousands of years ago in Greece, during the Battle of Thermopylae. The Greek soldiers, led by King Leonidas and his 300 Spartans, faced a much larger Persian army. Knowing they were outnumbered, the Greeks chose a narrow mountain pass to defend. Although this wasn't exactly a tall hill, it was a small, tight space surrounded by high rocks. The Greeks positioned themselves here to force the Persian army to approach in smaller groups, rather than all at once. This way, the

Spartans could fight fewer Persians at a time, using the high ground and tight path to their advantage. They held their position for days, even against a huge force, showing that picking the right terrain and holding it can make a big difference, even against powerful armies.

In ancient China, many generals also understood the power of defending the high ground. Sun Tzu, a famous Chinese military strategist, wrote about it in his famous book, *The Art of War*. He explained that being on high ground gives soldiers a better view of the battlefield, helping them spot enemy movements before they're too close. Ancient Chinese armies often built watchtowers on hills or mountains, allowing them to see enemy soldiers approaching from far away. When the enemy did try to attack uphill, Chinese defenders could shoot arrows down from their elevated position, making it hard for the attackers to get close. This strategy was especially effective along the Great Wall of China, which stretches over mountains and hills. By building the wall on high ground, the Chinese defenders could spot invaders and use the natural advantage of height to protect their land.

Ancient castles and forts were also often built on high ground for defense. In medieval Europe, castles were usually placed on top of hills or cliffs. This way, if an enemy army wanted to capture the castle, they had to climb up the hill while the defenders inside the castle could easily see them coming. Defenders could pour boiling water, oil, or stones down on the attackers, making it very hard to reach the castle walls. Many castles even had tall towers that allowed archers to shoot arrows from above, where they were safer from enemy attacks. With thick stone walls and high ground, these castles became very hard to conquer, and many could hold out for weeks or even months against large armies.

Another famous battle where high ground made a big difference was the Battle of Hastings in 1066. This battle happened in England, where the English soldiers took a strong position on top of a hill. They used a formation called a "shield wall," standing side by side with their shields raised to block the attackers. The attacking army, led by William the Conqueror, had to fight uphill, making it tough for them to break through the English defenses. The high ground helped the English soldiers protect themselves from the attackers' arrows and charges. Although the English eventually lost the battle, they were able to hold their ground for hours and inflict heavy losses on the enemy, showing just how powerful high ground can be when used correctly.

Defending high ground was also common in battles across Asia. Samurai warriors in Japan, for example, often chose hilltops or mountain passes as places to defend themselves against enemies. Japan's landscape has many mountains, so samurai used the natural geography to their advantage. In one famous battle, the samurai leader Minamoto no Yoshitsune defended a mountain pass, using his knowledge of the terrain to position his troops carefully. When the enemy tried to charge up the mountain, the samurai warriors held their ground and used their bows to strike the enemy from above, weakening them before they even reached the top. By choosing high ground, Yoshitsune was able to use fewer warriors to hold back a larger force.

High ground doesn't just give defenders a physical advantage; it also affects the way soldiers feel. When soldiers are positioned above their enemies, they often feel more confident and in control. Looking down at an approaching enemy can boost the defenders' morale because they know the attackers will struggle to reach them. On the other hand, attacking soldiers may feel nervous or scared when they have to climb up, knowing that they're vulnerable to attacks from above. This psychological edge can make a big difference in a battle, as soldiers who feel confident and safe are more likely to fight well and stay strong.

In ancient times, armies also used high ground to set traps. They would hide soldiers on top of hills or in forests along high cliffs. When the enemy passed through the area below, the hidden soldiers would attack from above. This tactic, called an ambush, made it hard for the enemy to fight back, especially if they didn't expect an attack from that direction. In battles, ambushes from high ground were common because they combined the element of surprise with the advantage of height. Armies in many parts of the world used these ambush tactics to defend their land and stop invading forces.

One of the most famous leaders to use high ground was Alexander the Great, a brilliant military commander from ancient Macedonia. He often chose high ground to set up his camps and position his troops. By doing this, Alexander could see enemy movements and plan his attacks more effectively. In one battle, he took the high ground on a ridge above his enemies, allowing him to control the fight and win with fewer soldiers. His use of high ground helped him conquer vast lands and become one of the most successful leaders in history.

In every part of the world, from Europe to Africa to the Americas, ancient armies used high ground as a smart way to defend their lands. The natural elevation made it easier to hold off attackers, spot enemies from far away, and launch attacks with a better chance of winning. This is why so many forts, castles, and even ancient villages were built on hilltops or cliffs. High ground wasn't just a place to fight; it was a place of safety and strength. By controlling the high ground, ancient warriors could protect their people, guard important areas, and even gain the respect and fear of their enemies.

The advantage of high ground has been so useful that it's still important in modern times. Today's military forces often use hills or elevated places for lookout posts or to place important equipment. Even in sports and games, being in the higher position can give players an edge. High ground has proven, over and over again, to be one of the best defenses, making it a timeless strategy that has helped shape the outcomes of battles throughout history.

Chapter 4: The Use of Camouflage

Imagine you're playing hide-and-seek, trying to find the perfect hiding spot where no one will notice you. If you're wearing bright colors, it might be hard to hide, but if you're dressed in green and brown and crouched in tall grass or near trees, you're more likely to stay hidden. This idea of blending into the surroundings to avoid being seen is called camouflage. In the animal kingdom, many creatures like chameleons, deer, and tigers use camouflage naturally. But people also learned that they could use camouflage in battle to hide from enemies, making it one of the most useful tricks in military history. By carefully choosing colors, patterns, and positions, soldiers could stay hidden, protect themselves, and sometimes surprise their enemies.

Camouflage has been used for thousands of years, and early armies understood its importance even without the technology and materials we have today. Ancient hunters, who had to get close to animals without scaring them, used basic camouflage to avoid being seen. They wore animal skins or clothes made from plants, and they painted their bodies with mud or clay to match their surroundings. Over time, these same techniques made their way into warfare. Soldiers fighting in fields, forests, and even deserts began using materials from their surroundings—like leaves, mud, and branches—to cover themselves and stay hidden. They learned that being seen less often could mean the difference between life and death in battle.

During the Napoleonic Wars in the early 19th century, camouflage wasn't widely used because soldiers often wore bright uniforms. Back then, it was common to see soldiers in colorful uniforms—red, blue, and white—that showed off their loyalty to their country. These uniforms looked impressive and made it easy for generals to see where their troops were on the battlefield. However, as weapons became more advanced and battles started to happen over longer distances, it became clear that standing out wasn't always safe. Imagine trying to hide on a battlefield while wearing bright red—it would be nearly impossible. Soldiers soon realized that blending into the background made them much safer and helped them avoid enemy attacks.

The concept of camouflage became especially important during World War I. The landscape of war changed drastically as soldiers fought in trenches—long, narrow ditches dug into the ground for protection. Since these battles often took place in open fields, hiding was difficult. Soldiers needed ways to blend in, so they started wearing uniforms in shades of brown, green, and gray, which helped them disappear against the muddy, grassy, and often smoky battlefield. Special units called "camoufleurs" were created, and these soldiers were responsible for finding new ways to keep soldiers hidden. They painted uniforms, tanks, and even cannons in patterns that mimicked the surrounding land, and they placed branches, leaves, and other natural materials around their positions to create makeshift cover.

In World War II, camouflage became even more advanced. By this time, armies had discovered that different types of camouflage were needed for different environments. For example, soldiers fighting in forests used camouflage with shades of green and brown, while those in deserts used sand-colored patterns. In snowy areas, soldiers wore white to blend in with the snow. During this time, many military leaders understood that if they could hide their soldiers, vehicles, and equipment, they'd have a much better chance of success in battles. They even used something called "dazzle camouflage" on ships—brightly colored patterns that looked almost like zigzags or stripes. Dazzle camouflage didn't hide the ships, but it confused enemy submarines about their direction, making it harder for them to aim correctly.

Camouflage wasn't just limited to soldiers and equipment. During both World Wars, armies also used camouflage to protect important buildings, roads, and even entire towns. For example, in World War II, the British tried to hide a large airplane factory from enemy planes. They painted the roofs to look like fields from above and added fake trees and bushes around it. Some areas even had fake houses or roads that made them look like small villages instead of military targets. The idea was to trick enemy pilots into flying right past without realizing they were near something important. In a way, this was like creating a large-scale hiding spot, making it hard for the enemy to locate their targets.

In the jungles of Southeast Asia, during wars like the Vietnam War, camouflage was used in some of the most challenging environments imaginable. The dense forests, filled with trees, vines, and thick underbrush, were the perfect place to hide. Soldiers wore green and brown uniforms and painted their faces to match the leaves and shadows around them. They also learned to move slowly and quietly, becoming almost invisible in the jungle. Sometimes, they would use natural materials like leaves, grass, and mud to cover their equipment, so even things like helmets and guns looked like part of the forest. The soldiers who were skilled in this kind of camouflage were often called "guerrilla fighters," and they used their knowledge of the land and camouflage to surprise their enemies, often appearing suddenly and disappearing just as quickly.

One of the more creative uses of camouflage has been in sniping. A sniper is a soldier who is trained to shoot from a long distance, and staying hidden is essential to their job. Snipers use something called a "ghillie suit," which is a special outfit made to look like leaves, branches, or grass. These suits are designed so that the sniper can lie in one spot and blend in perfectly with the surroundings. A well-trained sniper can stay still and hidden for hours, waiting for the right moment to take a shot without being seen. Ghillie suits have been used in many wars and continue to be a key part of camouflage for snipers today.

Camouflage is still used in modern warfare, but technology has made it even more advanced. Now, instead of just using colors and patterns, armies have developed materials that can change appearance. Some new types of camouflage fabrics can mimic the colors around them or even use digital patterns that break up the outline of a soldier's body, making them harder to spot. In some cases, scientists are even experimenting with materials that can reflect the scenery, almost like an invisibility cloak, to help soldiers hide better than ever.

Animals, of course, have inspired many of these camouflage techniques. Think about how a tiger's stripes help it blend into the grass and shadows of the jungle or how an octopus can change colors to match the coral and rocks underwater. Military camouflage designers study these animals to create new patterns that work just as well in deserts, forests, and other environments. For example, digital camouflage—small, square patterns that break up shapes—was inspired by nature and has become one of the most popular styles in modern military uniforms.

In addition to colors and patterns, camouflage also includes the use of shadows and sounds. Soldiers know that even if they are well hidden, a shadow or a sudden noise can give away their position. This is why they often move quietly and try to stay in shaded areas, where it's harder for enemies to spot them. In ancient times, soldiers were trained to stay silent, even during ambushes, because the smallest sound could ruin their cover. Modern soldiers learn similar techniques and may even camouflage their equipment to avoid reflections or anything shiny that might catch the enemy's eye.

Camouflage isn't just used in war; it's also common in outdoor activities like hunting, birdwatching, and even sports. Hunters wear camouflage clothing to get closer to animals, while photographers use it to capture pictures of wildlife without scaring it away. Some athletes use camouflage paint on their equipment to make it harder for opponents to spot certain moves in sports like paintball. Camouflage has become so popular that you'll even see it in fashion, with camouflage designs appearing on clothes, backpacks, and other everyday items.

The use of camouflage shows how creativity and understanding of nature can make a big difference in keeping people safe and giving them an advantage. From ancient times to the modern day, the art of blending in has helped armies win battles, protect important places, and even inspire designs for clothing and outdoor gear. Camouflage has truly become a part of life, going beyond the battlefield to become an essential skill for both people and animals who want to stay hidden.

Chapter 5: The Importance of Spies

Imagine you're part of a secret team trying to win a game, but the other team is much stronger and has more players. If you know their strategy in advance, like where they're hiding or which moves they plan to make, you'd have a better chance of winning. That's where spies come in—they gather information that's hidden from everyone else. Throughout history, spies have been some of the most important people in battles and wars because they bring back secret plans, hidden weaknesses, and vital information that can change the outcome of a conflict. Having spies has been like having an extra, hidden advantage, helping armies make smarter decisions and stay one step ahead of their enemies. The importance of spies goes back thousands of years and is still a key part of military strategy today.

In ancient times, before advanced technology, getting information about what the enemy was doing was much harder than it is now. Armies couldn't rely on satellite images, drones, or radios. Instead, they had to send people secretly into enemy territories to watch, listen, and sometimes even steal plans. Spies were often trained to disguise themselves so they wouldn't look like soldiers. They might dress like regular townspeople, traders, or even servants, so they could get close to important people without being noticed. Once they were inside enemy territory, they would try to learn anything useful that could help their side win the battle. If they found out about a sneak attack or discovered where the enemy was hiding their supplies, they'd hurry back to their own leaders to share this critical information.

One famous example of spies in action was during the Persian Wars between the Greeks and the Persians. The Greeks were facing a much larger army and needed every advantage they could find. They sent spies into the Persian camp to learn about their plans and find out where they were vulnerable. By doing this, the Greeks learned about the Persians' weaknesses and how they moved their troops, giving the

Greeks a better chance in battles like the famous Battle of Marathon. Spies didn't just gather information—they also spread false information to trick the enemy. In some cases, Greek spies would spread rumors or set traps to confuse the Persian soldiers, making them second-guess their plans and leaving them unsure of what to expect.

In ancient China, spies were a crucial part of military strategy. The famous military strategist Sun Tzu, who wrote *The Art of War*, emphasized the importance of using spies in battle. He believed that knowing your enemy's plans could give you a huge advantage, and he encouraged leaders to use spies to gain this insight. Sun Tzu described five different types of spies, each with a unique role. For example, he mentioned local spies—people who already lived in the enemy's land and could report back with what they observed. He also spoke about "double agents," spies who pretend to be loyal to one side but actually work for the other. Double agents are especially tricky because they send false information to their enemies, while secretly helping their own side. Sun Tzu's ideas about spies were so valuable that many military leaders, even today, still study his strategies to learn how to use spies effectively.

During the American Revolutionary War, spies played a big role in helping the Americans win independence from Britain. One of the most famous spy networks was the Culper Spy Ring, which worked secretly to gather information about British troop movements and plans. The spies in this group used special codes, hidden messages, and even invisible ink to share information. They were so careful that even if one spy got caught, the others wouldn't be discovered. One of the main leaders of the Culper Spy Ring was a man named Benjamin Tallmadge, who was an officer in the American army. He organized a network of trusted friends who could move in and out of British-controlled areas without being noticed. The information they collected helped George Washington, the leader of the American forces, make smarter decisions and avoid surprise attacks.

Another famous spy during the American Revolution was Nathan Hale, a young man who volunteered to go behind enemy lines to gather information about the British army. Sadly, Hale was caught by the British and executed for being a spy. Before his death, he famously said, "I only regret that I have but one life to lose for my country." Hale became an American hero, and his bravery inspired many others to take on the dangerous job of spying. Even though spies risked their lives, they knew that their work was essential to the cause of independence, and they were willing to do whatever it took to help their country.

In the Civil War, spies were again crucial for both the Union (the North) and the Confederacy (the South). One famous spy for the South was Rose O'Neal Greenhow, a socialite in Washington, D.C., who gathered information from Northern politicians and passed it along to the Confederate army. Rose was able to charm important people, making them trust her and share secrets without realizing she was a spy. She passed on information that helped the Confederates win some of the early battles. Eventually, the Union caught her and put her in prison, but her work as a spy showed just how powerful one person with the right information could be.

During World War I and World War II, spying became more organized and sophisticated. Governments set up entire agencies focused just on gathering intelligence, which is another word for information. In World War II, the British had a secret organization called the MI6, and the Americans formed the OSS, which later became the CIA. These groups worked on training spies, creating secret codes, and finding new ways to collect information. One of the most famous spies of this era was a woman named Virginia Hall. She was an American who worked for the British to gather information on the Germans in France. Hall was so good at hiding her identity that the Germans called her "The Limping Lady" because she had a wooden leg, but they could never catch her. She organized resistance fighters, helped them sabotage German equipment, and sent valuable information back to the Allies. Her courage and skill made her one of the most important spies in the war.

One of the most secretive projects during World War II was the Enigma code-breaking operation. The Germans used a complex machine called the Enigma to send coded messages, believing it was unbreakable. However, a group of British code-breakers, led by a brilliant mathematician named Alan Turing, managed to crack the code. By breaking the Enigma code, the Allies could read German messages and learn about their plans in advance. This information helped them win key battles and eventually win the war. Although Turing and his team weren't spies in the traditional sense, their work showed how powerful intelligence gathering could be.

In addition to human spies, animals have even been used in spying missions. During World War II, for instance, pigeons were trained to carry secret messages in small capsules attached to their legs. These birds could fly over enemy lines and deliver messages without being detected. Dolphins and other sea animals have also been trained in modern times to help with underwater spying. They can find hidden mines or even detect submarines. This use of animals as "spies" shows how creative intelligence agencies can be when they need to get information.

In modern times, spying has become even more advanced with the help of technology. Today, satellites in space can take pictures of enemy bases, and drones can fly over battle zones to gather information. Computers can be used to hack into enemy systems and steal valuable information. This kind of electronic spying is sometimes called "cyber espionage." Spies today don't always have to sneak around in disguise or hide in enemy territory. Instead, they might sit at a computer, collecting information from far away. But despite all the technology, human spies are still important because they can understand complex situations, build relationships, and gather information that computers can't find.

Spying also involves sending false information to the enemy, a tactic called "disinformation." During World War II, the Allies created a fake army to trick the Germans. They built inflatable tanks, trucks, and even tents that looked real from the air. They spread false messages to make the Germans think this fake army was going to attack a different location. This trick was called Operation Fortitude, and it worked. The Germans were fooled and moved their troops to the wrong place, helping the real Allied forces succeed in the D-Day invasion of Normandy.

The importance of spies goes beyond just battles and wars. In peacetime, spies still gather information to protect their countries from threats. Intelligence agencies keep an eye on possible dangers like terrorist groups, secret weapons programs, or cyberattacks. Spies work quietly, often without anyone knowing who they are, to keep their country safe from hidden dangers. Although spying can be risky and challenging, spies are proud of the role they play in protecting their people.

Spies have had a huge impact on history, helping leaders make decisions, win battles, and even change the course of wars. By gathering information, spreading disinformation, and sometimes risking everything for a mission, spies use their skills to keep their side safe and strong. Through ancient times, major wars, and even modern times with advanced technology, spies have proven just how powerful hidden knowledge can be. They are like the unseen players in history, helping shape the world while remaining in the shadows.

Chapter 6: Fortresses and Strongholds

Imagine you're in a castle high on a hill, with thick stone walls all around, sturdy towers at each corner, and a deep moat below. You feel safe because you're protected from every side, with guards keeping watch and supplies stored up for a long stay. This kind of strong, defensive place is called a fortress or a stronghold. Throughout history, people have built fortresses to protect themselves, their families, and their communities from enemies. These fortresses were made to keep attackers out and to give defenders a secure base to fight from. Strongholds were more than just buildings; they were like entire communities with homes, supplies, and places for soldiers to defend against invaders. Let's dive into the history of fortresses and strongholds and learn how they've been used in battles and wars to protect and defend.

Long ago, people lived in small groups or tribes. When conflicts started to arise, people realized that they needed better ways to defend themselves. At first, people used natural places like caves, steep hills, or areas surrounded by rivers for protection. But as battles became more common, they began building their own strongholds. Early fortresses were simple and were often built from materials like wood and mud. For instance, ancient hillforts in Europe had large wooden fences surrounding them, while people living in desert areas used mud bricks to build thick walls. Even though these early forts were basic, they made a huge difference in safety. When attackers approached, villagers would hurry inside the walls and defend their homes from behind these barriers.

As time went on, fortresses became more advanced. Stone, which is much stronger than wood, became the preferred building material. Stone walls were nearly impossible to break down with early weapons, so these stone fortresses were incredibly tough. Castles began to appear in places like medieval Europe, where kings, lords, and knights needed secure places to rule and defend against rivals. Castles weren't just defensive buildings; they were also homes where royalty and nobility lived, complete with luxurious rooms, grand dining halls, and beautiful decorations. But the main purpose was always defense. Thick stone walls, often several feet wide, kept enemies out, and towers provided a high vantage point for watching over the land.

One famous early fortress is the Great Wall of China, which was built over many centuries by different Chinese dynasties. The Great Wall stretches thousands of miles across northern China and was originally built to protect against invading tribes like the Mongols. It wasn't a single fortress but a series of walls, towers, and fortifications that worked together as a giant stronghold to protect China. Soldiers patrolled the wall and kept watch for invaders, and large beacons or smoke signals were used to send messages quickly from one part of the wall to another. The Great Wall is one of the most impressive examples of defensive architecture in history and shows just how seriously people took the idea of defending their land.

In Europe during the Middle Ages, castles were everywhere. They were built not only by kings but also by wealthy nobles who wanted to protect their land and people. Castles like these were designed with clever features to make them harder to attack. For instance, many castles had moats—wide ditches filled with water—around their walls. Moats made it difficult for attackers to reach the walls, and anyone trying to swim across would be an easy target for archers. Castles often had drawbridges that could be raised or lowered over the moat. When danger was near, the drawbridge would be pulled up, closing off the entrance completely.

The entrance to a castle was often protected by a heavy, iron-covered door called a portcullis. If enemies got through the outer gate, they'd face the portcullis, which could be dropped suddenly to trap them inside. Even if attackers got through the portcullis, they would enter a narrow, winding passage that forced them to slow down, making it easier for defenders to stop them. Castle designers also created "murder holes" in the ceiling of these passages. Defenders above could drop rocks, hot oil, or arrows down through these holes, making it extremely dangerous for any enemy inside.

At the top of the castle walls, soldiers used battlements, which are gaps in the wall that allowed defenders to shoot arrows while staying protected. Some castles had towers at each corner or along the walls, where lookouts could keep watch for miles around. Towers gave defenders an advantage because they were high up, allowing them to see enemies approaching from a long distance. Some castles even had special towers called "watchtowers" on nearby hills or high ground to spot enemies earlier. By seeing the enemy early, defenders could prepare for an attack before the invaders got too close.

Fortresses and strongholds didn't just protect people; they also stored supplies. Since fortresses were often surrounded by the enemy during a siege, the people inside needed food, water, weapons, and other supplies to last them for weeks or even months. Castles had large storage rooms filled with food, and many had their own wells to provide fresh water. Animals like chickens and pigs were kept inside the fortress so the defenders would have fresh meat if they needed it. Fortresses were like little cities, built to survive on their own for long periods, even if no one could get in or out.

During a siege, when an enemy surrounded a fortress, attackers tried many strategies to get inside. They might use battering rams—huge wooden beams—to smash down gates. They also built tall towers, called siege towers, that could be rolled up to the fortress walls, allowing soldiers to climb up and attack defenders on the wall. Catapults and trebuchets, which were large machines that hurled heavy stones or flaming objects, were used to break down walls or frighten the people inside. But the thick walls and clever design of many fortresses made them strong against these attacks, and the defenders often held out for a long time.

One legendary fortress was the Krak des Chevaliers in modern-day Syria, built during the Crusades. The Crusaders, European knights who fought to control the Holy Land, built this castle to defend against Muslim armies. With its thick walls, tall towers, and high position on a hill, Krak des Chevaliers was almost impossible to capture. It became one of the most famous fortresses of its time, known for withstanding many sieges. The people inside could see enemies approaching from far away and had enough supplies to hold out for a long time. Krak des Chevaliers shows just how effective a strong fortress could be at keeping attackers at bay.

In Japan, samurai warriors built their own style of strongholds called castles, which were slightly different from European castles. Japanese castles often had curved, layered roofs that were both beautiful and defensive. They also used stone bases to make it hard for attackers to climb up, and the pathways leading to the castle were often narrow and winding, forcing attackers to move slowly and making them easy targets. Himeji Castle is a famous example of a Japanese castle. Its bright white walls and layered design earned it the nickname "White Heron Castle." Like European castles, Japanese castles were built for both beauty and defense, providing a safe place for samurai warriors and their lords.

Fortresses continued to be important even as weapons became more powerful. In the 1600s and 1700s, guns and cannons changed how fortresses were designed. Old-style castles with high walls were no longer as effective, since cannons could blast through them. To adapt, architects began designing lower, thicker walls called "star forts." These forts had a star-like shape with points sticking out in different directions. This shape allowed soldiers to defend from multiple angles, making it harder for attackers to get close. Star forts became popular in Europe and America, especially during wars like the American Revolution.

Even in modern times, strongholds and fortresses are used, although they look much different. During World War I and World War II, soldiers dug trenches, bunkers, and underground fortifications to protect themselves from powerful weapons. For example, in France, the Maginot Line was a massive defensive line of bunkers and tunnels built along the border with Germany. It was designed to stop any invasion and had everything from living quarters to hospitals underground. The bunkers were made of reinforced concrete, and many were deep underground, safe from bombs and artillery. Even though the Maginot Line wasn't completely successful, it showed how important fortresses still were in modern warfare.

Today, technology has changed the way we think about fortresses. While we don't often see large stone castles being built, the idea of a stronghold still exists in military bases, underground bunkers, and secure facilities around the world. Some countries even have hidden bases inside mountains or under the ocean to protect against attacks. Modern "fortresses" use steel, concrete, and high-tech security systems instead of stone walls and moats. They are protected with cameras, alarms, and even automated weapons. However, the basic idea is still the same—to create a safe place where people and supplies can be protected against any kind of attack.

Fortresses and strongholds have played a huge role in history, giving people a safe place to defend themselves and survive attacks. From ancient forts made of mud and wood to stone castles with moats and drawbridges, from star forts that could withstand cannon fire to modern bunkers deep underground, strongholds have shown how creative and determined people can be when it comes to defense. These powerful structures remind us of the courage and determination of those who defended them, holding off enemies to protect the people and land they loved.

Chapter 7: Lightning Speed Attacks

Imagine you're playing a game, and instead of moving slowly and waiting for the other team to make the first move, you suddenly charge forward with all your strength, taking the other team by surprise before they even know what's happening. This is what a lightning speed attack is like in real battles—a sudden, fast, and powerful strike that catches the enemy off guard and doesn't give them any time to react. Throughout history, commanders and armies have used lightning speed attacks to overwhelm their enemies and gain the upper hand in wars. These attacks require careful planning, but once they start, they move quickly, like a flash of lightning, creating chaos for the enemy.

One of the reasons lightning speed attacks are so powerful is that they don't give the enemy time to organize. Normally, before a battle, both sides set up their forces, choose their best positions, and get their defenses ready. But when a lightning attack begins, the defenders don't have time to do any of that. They might still be getting into position, or maybe they haven't even realized the enemy is near. By the time they figure out what's going on, the attackers are already on top of them, causing confusion and panic. For the attackers, moving fast and striking first means they can sometimes win the battle even before it properly begins.

In ancient times, speed was one of the greatest advantages a commander could have. One famous leader who loved using fast attacks was Alexander the Great. Alexander was a brilliant general who conquered vast areas of land in a very short time. Part of his success came from his army's ability to move quickly and strike hard. Alexander's soldiers didn't wait for the enemy to attack first; instead, they would charge forward with energy and confidence. For example, in the Battle of Gaugamela against the Persian Empire, Alexander used a lightning speed attack to break through the Persian lines. His army was outnumbered, but by moving quickly and catching the Persians off guard, he was able to defeat a much larger force. His fast attacks surprised his enemies and made it almost impossible for them to keep up with his movements.

Another famous example of lightning speed attacks comes from the Mongols, a fierce group of warriors from Central Asia. Led by Genghis Khan, the Mongols created one of the largest empires in history, and they did it largely by moving with incredible speed. The Mongol soldiers were skilled horsemen and could travel long distances quickly. When they attacked a city or an enemy army, they moved so fast that defenders often had no idea they were coming until it was too late. The Mongols would surround a city or a camp within hours, giving the enemy no chance to prepare. This quick movement and surprise gave the Mongols a huge advantage, and they were able to conquer many powerful armies and capture cities in record time.

In modern history, one of the most famous uses of lightning speed attacks was during World War II, when the Germans used a strategy called "Blitzkrieg," which means "lightning war" in German. Blitzkrieg was a new way of fighting that combined speed, surprise, and powerful attacks. Instead of attacking slowly or waiting for the enemy to make the first move, the Germans would launch a sudden and intense attack. They used tanks, planes, and infantry (soldiers on foot) together in a coordinated strike. First, their planes would bomb enemy positions, creating confusion and fear. Then, tanks would roll in quickly, breaking through the enemy's defenses. Finally, soldiers would follow to secure the area. The entire attack happened so quickly that the defenders couldn't keep up, and many surrendered almost immediately.

Blitzkrieg worked so well that the Germans conquered large parts of Europe in a matter of months. In Poland, France, and other countries, the Blitzkrieg strategy allowed the Germans to overwhelm their enemies before they had time to organize. This speed and surprise made the German army seem unstoppable at the beginning of the war. Blitzkrieg was a perfect example of how lightning speed attacks can change the course of a battle or even a war by catching the enemy off guard and hitting them with a force they weren't prepared for.

But lightning speed attacks aren't only about rushing forward; they also require clever planning and organization. A commander has to know exactly where to strike and when to do it. If they charge too early or in the wrong direction, they could end up in a dangerous position. For example, if an army uses a lightning speed attack but isn't careful, they could run right into a trap or end up separated from their main group, making it easy for the enemy to surround them. That's why a lot of thought goes into these attacks before they happen. The commanders need to study the enemy, look for weaknesses, and choose the right moment to launch the attack.

Napoleon Bonaparte, the famous French general and emperor, was another leader who used fast, powerful attacks. Napoleon's army was famous for its ability to move quickly and hit hard. Napoleon would study the enemy and then strike suddenly, focusing all his strength on one part of their line. By doing this, he could break through their defenses and cause confusion. One of his most famous battles was the Battle of Austerlitz, where he faced two powerful armies at once, the Russian and Austrian forces. Napoleon used a fast, surprise attack to split their armies and defeat them one by one. His lightning speed attack allowed him to win a great victory, even though he was outnumbered.

In addition to armies, special forces and small groups of elite soldiers often use lightning speed attacks to achieve their missions. These soldiers are highly trained to move quickly, strike hard, and disappear before the enemy even knows they were there. Special forces units like the U.S. Navy SEALs or the British SAS are famous for their lightning-fast raids. They might be sent to capture an important target, rescue hostages, or destroy a key enemy base. Because they move so quickly, these small teams can accomplish important missions that larger, slower armies might not be able to. In these cases, a lightning speed attack means going in, completing the mission, and getting out before the enemy has time to respond.

Another example of a lightning speed attack can be found in the history of samurai warriors in Japan. Samurai were highly trained and disciplined fighters who valued speed, surprise, and precision in battle. One of their favorite tactics was a quick, surprise attack called an "ambush." Samurai would often hide along a road or in a forest, waiting for the perfect moment to strike. When their enemy came close, they would charge out with lightning speed, surprising and overpowering their opponents. This tactic was very effective because it didn't give the enemy time to prepare, and the samurai could often win the battle in a matter of minutes. Samurai attacks were not only fast but also carefully planned, showing how important strategy is in making a lightning speed attack work.

In naval battles, speed and surprise are also important. During World War II, the Japanese navy used fast, small boats called torpedo boats to attack larger enemy ships. These torpedo boats would approach quickly, fire their torpedoes, and then speed away before the larger ship had time to react. This lightning speed approach allowed the smaller boats to fight against much bigger opponents by catching them off guard. The speed of the torpedo boats gave them an advantage, and they could often avoid being hit by the slower, larger guns of the big ships. This tactic showed how even in the vast ocean, speed and surprise could turn the tide of battle.

Lightning speed attacks have also been used in air battles. Fighter pilots in World War I and World War II would sometimes use a tactic called "hit-and-run," where they would swoop down quickly, fire at enemy planes or targets on the ground, and then fly away before the enemy could strike back. These quick attacks allowed fighter pilots to take out enemy planes or damage important targets without staying in one place for too long, which made it harder for enemy gunners to aim and shoot them down. This tactic was especially important for pilots who were outnumbered or facing strong anti-aircraft defenses.

Today, lightning speed attacks are still used in modern warfare, though technology has changed how they're carried out. Drones, for example, can be used for surprise attacks because they can fly in quickly, strike, and leave before the enemy even sees them coming. Cyberattacks, where hackers quickly break into an enemy's computer systems, are also a form of lightning speed attack in the digital world. These attacks are fast, surprising, and can cause a lot of damage if the enemy isn't prepared. Whether in the air, on the ground, or in cyberspace, the principle of striking fast and hard is still a powerful way to gain an advantage.

One of the challenges of a lightning speed attack is maintaining communication and coordination. When armies or groups are moving quickly, it's easy for them to get separated or lose track of each other. If communication breaks down, the attackers can get confused or even attack the wrong targets. That's why lightning speed attacks are often led by experienced leaders who know how to keep their troops organized, even in the chaos of a fast-moving battle. These leaders have to be calm and decisive, guiding their soldiers with quick commands and making sure everyone stays focused on the mission.

Lightning speed attacks have proven over and over again to be one of the most effective ways to surprise and overwhelm an enemy. By moving quickly, attacking suddenly, and keeping the enemy off balance, armies throughout history have used this tactic to win battles against all odds. Whether it was Alexander the Great charging forward with his army, the Mongols sweeping across Asia with incredible speed, or modern special forces completing missions in the blink of an eye, lightning speed attacks show that sometimes the best defense is a fast, bold offense. These attacks remind us that in both games and battles, sometimes the best way to win is to strike quickly, leaving the enemy stunned and unable to respond.

Chapter 8: The Art of Retreating

In battles, you might think that the only way to win is by charging forward and defeating the enemy. But sometimes, the smartest thing a commander can do is to retreat—to pull back and get away from a dangerous situation. Retreating might sound like giving up, but in the art of war, it can actually be a very wise and strategic choice. The art of retreating is about knowing when to step back, how to protect your soldiers while you do it, and using a retreat to come back stronger or avoid a terrible loss. Some of the greatest generals in history have used retreats as part of their battle plans, turning what seemed like a defeat into a chance to fight another day, gather more resources, or come up with a new plan.

One of the most important reasons for retreating is to save the lives of soldiers. When commanders see that their side is losing, or if the enemy has some advantage that makes winning impossible, they might decide to pull their troops back rather than risk losing everyone in a hopeless fight. This isn't about running away in fear; it's about protecting their people so that they can continue fighting another time. A smart retreat can preserve the army, allowing it to recover and try again in the future. In war, soldiers are a precious resource, and keeping them safe can be more valuable than any single battle victory.

Ancient armies often used retreats as part of their strategy. For instance, the Roman army was known for its discipline and clever tactics. If the Romans found themselves in a difficult position, they would sometimes retreat in an organized, step-by-step way, where each part of the army would move back while the others held their ground, protecting the entire group as they withdrew. This allowed them to keep their soldiers safe while also preventing the enemy from attacking them as they left. The Romans were skilled at organizing their troops in such a way that they could pull back without panicking, which was key to a successful retreat. A disorderly retreat could lead to chaos, where soldiers might scatter, making them easy targets for the enemy. The Romans showed that a controlled, organized retreat could be as powerful as an attack.

One famous historical retreat was made by Alexander the Great. Known for his incredible victories and his daring charges, Alexander was usually on the attack. But in the mountains of India, he faced an enemy that was unfamiliar with his fighting style and knew the area much better than his own soldiers. Realizing that continuing the fight would only lead to heavy losses, Alexander ordered a retreat. However, instead of just running away, he arranged for part of his army to hold off the enemy while the rest withdrew in stages, making sure no one was left behind or in danger. This careful retreat allowed him to save his army, regroup, and eventually move on to other victories. By retreating wisely, Alexander avoided a disastrous defeat and was able to continue his conquests.

Another famous retreat happened during the American Revolutionary War. George Washington, the leader of the American forces, had to retreat many times during the early years of the war. In one famous instance, his army was trapped by the British near Brooklyn in New York. The British had a larger, stronger army, and it seemed like Washington's forces would be completely defeated. But Washington came up with a daring plan to retreat across the East River during the night. With the help of boats and a thick fog that kept the British from seeing them, Washington's soldiers quietly moved away from the battlefield and escaped. This retreat saved the American army and allowed them to continue fighting for independence. If Washington had stayed and fought, his forces would likely have been destroyed, and the American Revolution might have ended right then and there.

The art of retreating doesn't just mean pulling back when you're losing; it can also be used as a trick to fool the enemy. Sometimes, armies pretend to retreat, luring the enemy into a trap. This is called a "feigned retreat," and it has been used by many clever generals throughout history. For example, the Mongols, led by Genghis Khan, were experts at using feigned retreats to deceive their enemies. In one of their battles, the Mongols pretended to run away, making their enemies think they had won. But as the enemies chased after them, the Mongols suddenly turned around and attacked, catching the other side off guard. By pretending to retreat, they lured the enemy into a dangerous position, where they were easily defeated. This tactic requires excellent timing and discipline because the retreating soldiers have to stay organized and be ready to turn around and fight at a moment's notice.

One of the largest and most famous retreats in history happened during Napoleon Bonaparte's invasion of Russia in 1812. Napoleon, a brilliant military leader, led his army deep into Russia, hoping to capture the capital city, Moscow. Although he succeeded in reaching the city, he found it almost abandoned and without supplies. As winter set in, his soldiers began to suffer from cold and hunger. Realizing that staying in Russia would only lead to disaster, Napoleon ordered his army to retreat. However, the journey back was incredibly difficult. Russian soldiers and local fighters harassed the retreating French army, while the freezing weather and lack of food took a terrible toll on the soldiers. By the time Napoleon's army finally made it back to friendly territory, they had lost thousands of men. This retreat showed the risks of retreating under harsh conditions and how important it is to plan and prepare, even for a withdrawal.

Another example of a retreat used as a strategy comes from the Battle of Dunkirk during World War II. The German army was advancing quickly through Europe, and the British and French forces were trapped on the beaches of Dunkirk in France. With no way to escape by land, it seemed certain that the soldiers would be captured or killed. But the British came up with a bold plan to evacuate their troops across the English Channel. Boats of all kinds—from navy ships to fishing boats—were called in to rescue the soldiers. For days, the British and French soldiers held off the Germans while hundreds of thousands of troops were evacuated to safety. This retreat, known as the "Miracle of Dunkirk," saved the British army and allowed them to regroup and continue fighting. Although they had to leave behind a lot of equipment, saving the soldiers was more important, as they could be equipped again to fight later on.

In military history, retreats are often seen as moments of weakness, but they require as much courage and skill as an attack. Soldiers retreating have to stay calm, keep together, and follow orders to avoid being overrun by the enemy. A well-planned retreat takes a lot of discipline and strong leadership. It's not easy to pull back while an enemy is advancing, and it's especially challenging to keep soldiers focused and prevent panic. The key to a successful retreat is keeping everyone organized and moving in a coordinated way, so that the army doesn't become scattered and vulnerable.

Retreats can also give armies time to gather strength or call for reinforcements. By pulling back, a commander might be able to regroup with fresh soldiers, bring in supplies, or find a stronger position from which to fight. Sometimes, armies retreat to lure the enemy into a place where they have the advantage, like higher ground or a narrow pass. In these situations, a retreat isn't just about escaping; it's about positioning the army in a way that will help them win the next battle. By choosing the right place and time to make a stand, commanders can turn a retreat into a strategic advantage.

In Japan, samurai warriors also practiced the art of retreat. The samurai believed that it was honorable to retreat if it meant saving lives and fighting again with a better chance of winning. They understood that sometimes stepping back was wiser than rushing forward. The samurai valued strategy and believed that a smart retreat could be more effective than a brave but hopeless stand. Samurai leaders taught their warriors that retreating wasn't a sign of weakness, but rather a way to protect their clan and come back stronger.

Even today, the art of retreating is still used in modern warfare. Soldiers sometimes need to pull back to avoid heavy losses or to regroup for a stronger attack. For example, in modern conflicts, armies might retreat to safer positions when they come under heavy fire. They may also use armored vehicles or helicopters to quickly get out of dangerous situations, protecting the lives of their soldiers. In these situations, a well-planned retreat allows soldiers to stay safe and return to the battle when they are better prepared. Modern technology, like radio and satellite communication, helps commanders organize retreats more effectively by keeping troops connected even while moving quickly.

Retreating also has psychological benefits. By pulling back, a commander can reduce fear and stress among soldiers who might feel overwhelmed. A retreat can give troops a chance to rest, recover, and regain their confidence before facing the enemy again. For soldiers, knowing that retreat is an option can be reassuring, allowing them to fight more bravely because they trust that their leaders won't push them into an impossible situation. Knowing when to pull back is a sign of wisdom, showing that the commander values the lives of their soldiers and isn't willing to throw them into a hopeless battle.

In summary, the art of retreating is a valuable skill in warfare that goes beyond simply running away. A well-planned retreat can save lives, preserve resources, and give armies the chance to come back stronger and more prepared. Whether used to avoid defeat, to lure enemies into a trap, or to regroup and recover, retreating has proven to be a powerful strategy for both ancient and modern armies. From the disciplined withdrawals of the Romans to the feigned retreats of the Mongols, and from George Washington's daring escape to the "Miracle of Dunkirk," history shows that knowing when and how to retreat is just as important as knowing when to attack. The art of retreating is about balance, courage, and strategy, proving that sometimes the best way to win is by taking a step back today to make a stronger stand tomorrow.

Chapter 9: Deception on the Battlefield

Imagine you're playing a game of hide-and-seek, but instead of hiding in a single place, you create a clever plan to trick the seeker. Maybe you leave some clues leading them in the wrong direction or pretend to hide somewhere else to distract them. In battles throughout history, commanders and soldiers have used similar tricks to fool their enemies. This type of strategy is called deception, and it's all about using clever tricks, fake moves, and unexpected surprises to confuse the enemy and gain an advantage. Deception on the battlefield can be as important as a strong army or powerful weapons because it allows a smaller or weaker army to outsmart a larger one, making the enemy believe things that aren't true.

One of the main goals of deception in battle is to make the enemy think you're somewhere you're not. This can involve creating fake camps, leaving trails in certain directions, or even using dummies or decoys to make the enemy believe they're facing a much larger force. The goal is to confuse the enemy so they make mistakes, like dividing their forces, moving to the wrong place, or lowering their defenses. This kind of trickery has been used in battles for thousands of years, helping leaders win battles without needing a direct fight.

One famous example of battlefield deception is the story of the Trojan Horse. In ancient Greek mythology, the Greeks wanted to capture the city of Troy, but Troy had strong walls that were impossible to break through. After years of fighting, the Greeks decided to use deception. They pretended to give up and sail away, but left behind a large wooden horse outside the gates of Troy. The people of Troy thought it was a gift and brought it inside their city walls. But inside the horse, Greek soldiers were hiding! When night fell and the city was asleep, the soldiers climbed out of the horse, opened the gates, and let the Greek army into the city. This deception helped the Greeks finally conquer Troy, showing how a clever trick could succeed where brute force had failed.

Ancient Chinese military leader Sun Tzu, who wrote *The Art of War*, was a master of deception. Sun Tzu believed that one of the best ways to win a battle was to trick the enemy. He advised leaders to make the enemy believe that you're weak when you're strong and that you're near when you're actually far away. This way, the enemy would misjudge your abilities and make mistakes. Sun Tzu's ideas on deception have been used by many military leaders throughout history, as they understand that confusing the enemy can lead to victory. By appearing vulnerable or pretending to retreat, commanders could lure enemies into a trap or an ambush, where the real force would be waiting to strike.

Another famous example of deception in battle comes from Hannibal, a great Carthaginian general who lived around 200 BC. Hannibal is known for his incredible tactics in the Second Punic War against Rome. In one famous battle, the Battle of Cannae, Hannibal used a clever trick to defeat a much larger Roman army. He arranged his soldiers in a way that made it look like his forces were weaker in the middle. When the Romans attacked, they saw this "weak" center and charged forward, thinking they could break through. But this was exactly what Hannibal wanted. As the Romans pressed forward, Hannibal's troops on the sides closed in around them, surrounding the Roman soldiers completely. By using deception, Hannibal defeated a much larger army and won one of the greatest victories in ancient warfare.

In medieval times, deception on the battlefield continued to be a powerful tactic. Armies would sometimes light extra campfires at night to make it look like they had more soldiers than they actually did. They might also send a small group of soldiers to make noise, shout, and act like a large force, tricking the enemy into believing they were surrounded. These kinds of tricks would make the enemy nervous and uncertain, causing them to overestimate the size and strength of their opponents. By creating fear and confusion, a smaller force could sometimes scare off a larger enemy or even make them surrender without a fight.

During World War II, deception reached new levels with the help of technology and new strategies. One of the most famous examples of deception during this time was Operation Fortitude, part of the D-Day invasion in 1944. The Allies, including American, British, and Canadian forces, planned to invade Nazi-occupied France to begin liberating Europe from German control. However, they wanted to keep the exact location of the invasion a secret to surprise the Germans. To do this, they used a huge deception plan to make the Germans believe the invasion would happen at a different location. The Allies created fake tanks, airplanes, and even a fake army commanded by the famous General George Patton. They set up these fake forces in a place called Dover, across from Calais, which is where they wanted the Germans to think the attack would come from. They also used fake radio messages and double agents (spies who pretended to work for the Germans but were really helping the Allies) to spread false information. This trick worked so well that when the real invasion happened in Normandy, the Germans were caught off guard, and the Allied forces were able to make a successful landing. Operation Fortitude is one of the most famous examples of battlefield deception and shows how well-planned tricks can change the course of history.

Deception also works by hiding true intentions. For example, sometimes generals might move troops around to make it look like they're planning to attack one place when they're actually targeting another. By tricking the enemy into thinking the wrong location is their goal, they can weaken the enemy's defenses in the real target area. In the American Civil War, the Confederate general Robert E. Lee used this kind of deception many times. Lee would have his troops march in one direction, making it look like he was going to attack a certain city. Meanwhile, his real target was somewhere else. The Union forces would rush to defend the city they thought was under threat, leaving the real target undefended. This allowed Lee to strike where he wanted and gain an advantage despite having fewer soldiers.

Sometimes, deception doesn't involve tricking the enemy about your location or strength but instead uses psychological tricks. Commanders would use things like noise and confusion to scare the enemy or make them hesitate. Some armies would even dress up in enemy uniforms, pretending to be friendly forces to get close before launching an attack. While this tactic was risky and could backfire if discovered, it was sometimes used as a way to infiltrate enemy positions or cause confusion. By blending in or acting in unexpected ways, armies could sow fear and chaos, making it harder for the enemy to respond.

The use of camouflage is another important part of deception. By blending into their surroundings, soldiers and equipment can stay hidden from the enemy, allowing them to get close without being seen. This is especially important for scouts and snipers, who need to move close to enemy positions without revealing themselves. Camouflage has been used since ancient times, but it became much more advanced in the 20th century. Soldiers learned to cover themselves with leaves, paint their faces, and wear clothes that matched their environment. In World War I, artists even designed special camouflage patterns for tanks, ships, and airplanes, making it harder for enemies to spot them from a distance.

Fake signals and false information are also part of battlefield deception. In the days before modern technology, armies would sometimes use drummers or trumpeters to send signals that confused the enemy. If the enemy thought that the drumming or trumpeting meant the army was retreating, they might charge forward, only to find themselves walking into a trap. Later, in the 20th century, armies started using radio signals to send fake messages, tricking the enemy into thinking they were planning something different. Even today, electronic deception is used in military operations, where fake signals are sent to mislead enemy radar and communication systems.

In the modern era, technology has made deception even more sophisticated. Armies use "decoy" equipment, such as inflatable tanks and fake airplanes, to confuse enemy satellites and reconnaissance. These decoys look real from above, so when the enemy sees them on a radar or satellite image, they think they're seeing real military equipment. This kind of deception can trick the enemy into thinking an attack is coming from a certain direction, causing them to prepare in the wrong place. By using decoys, modern armies continue the ancient tradition of tricking the enemy with fake forces.

Another form of deception used today is cyber warfare. In cyber warfare, deception happens in the virtual world, where hackers can plant false information, create fake online activities, or make it look like something is happening that really isn't. For example, a cyberattack might make it look like a country's defenses are down, luring the enemy to attack, only for them to be met with a strong defense. This type of deception can confuse and mislead enemies, creating digital chaos instead of physical confusion.

Throughout history, the art of deception on the battlefield has shown that war is not only about strength but also about intelligence, creativity, and the ability to think several steps ahead. Commanders who mastered deception knew that making the enemy believe something false could be more powerful than facing them directly. Deception allows armies to create opportunities, weaken the enemy's confidence, and strike when they are least prepared. In many cases, a well-executed deception plan has been the deciding factor in a battle or even a war, showing that sometimes the best way to win isn't by being the strongest, but by being the smartest.

Chapter 10: Guerrilla Warfare Secrets

Guerrilla warfare is a type of fighting that's very different from the usual battles where two large armies face each other directly. Instead, guerrilla warfare is all about being sneaky, fast, and unpredictable. People who fight using guerrilla tactics often don't have the big, powerful weapons or large numbers of soldiers that an official army might have, so they rely on cleverness, surprise, and using their environment to outsmart their opponents. The goal of guerrilla fighters is not necessarily to defeat the enemy in one big battle but to slowly wear them down, causing confusion, frustration, and making it harder for the enemy to fight back over time. This style of fighting has been used for thousands of years by smaller forces to defend themselves against much stronger armies.

One of the key secrets of guerrilla warfare is the element of surprise. Guerrilla fighters usually operate in small groups and plan quick, unexpected attacks on their enemies. They might wait until the enemy is passing through a narrow valley, or they might strike in the middle of the night when the enemy is resting. Because they are often outnumbered, guerrilla fighters have to be very careful about when and where they attack. They try to hit the enemy when they least expect it, causing damage and confusion before quickly disappearing. This leaves the enemy frustrated and unsure of where or when they might be attacked next, which can lower their morale and make them anxious.

Another important secret of guerrilla warfare is using the terrain to their advantage. Guerrilla fighters are often very familiar with the area where they're fighting, whether it's dense forests, tall mountains, deserts, or jungles. By knowing the land well, they can hide in places where the enemy won't easily find them, like caves, thick trees, or high ridges. This knowledge also helps them move quickly and quietly, avoiding paths or roads where they might be spotted. Because the enemy often isn't as familiar with the area, they can get lost, trapped, or slowed down by difficult terrain. This gives guerrilla fighters a big advantage, allowing them to move easily while the enemy struggles to catch up or even find them.

A famous example of guerrilla warfare in history comes from ancient China with a strategist named Zhuge Liang. Zhuge Liang used clever tactics to defend his territory from powerful armies. One of his most famous tricks was the "empty city" tactic. When his city was about to be attacked, and he had very few soldiers to defend it, Zhuge Liang ordered that the gates of the city be opened wide, and he sat calmly on the city wall, playing a musical instrument. When the enemy army arrived and saw the open gates and calm scene, they thought it was a trap and decided not to attack. In reality, the city was almost defenseless, but Zhuge Liang's trick worked, and the city was saved without a fight. This is just one example of how guerrilla tactics rely on cleverness rather than brute strength.

Guerrilla warfare also involves disrupting the enemy's supplies. In a typical battle, armies need food, water, ammunition, and other supplies to keep fighting. Guerrilla fighters often don't try to destroy the enemy directly but instead focus on cutting off these supplies, making it difficult for the enemy to survive in the area. For example, guerrilla fighters might destroy bridges to stop supply trucks or set up traps along supply routes to make it dangerous for the enemy to bring in food and reinforcements. By doing this, they can weaken the enemy without facing them directly. When an enemy army starts to run low on supplies, they can become desperate, hungry, and much easier to defeat. This strategy is often more effective than attacking head-on, as it wears down the enemy over time.

One of the most famous guerrilla warfare leaders in history was General Vo Nguyen Giap from Vietnam. During the Vietnam War, he led his forces against the much larger and better-equipped American army. Giap understood that his forces could not win in a direct fight, so he used guerrilla tactics to his advantage. His soldiers, known as the Viet Cong, would hide in the dense jungles of Vietnam, using tunnels, ambushes, and hit-and-run attacks to confuse and exhaust the American troops. The Viet Cong built an extensive network of tunnels where they could hide, store supplies, and even set up small hospitals. These tunnels allowed them to disappear quickly after an attack, making it very difficult for the enemy to find them. The jungles also helped because they provided natural cover, making it hard for the American soldiers to spot the guerrilla fighters.

Using small groups is another secret to guerrilla warfare success. Rather than moving in large numbers like traditional armies, guerrilla fighters break up into small teams that are quick and flexible. These small groups can move through the countryside without being easily detected and can regroup at a different location whenever they need to. This makes them hard to pin down because, even if one group is found, the rest are still safe. Smaller groups can also carry out multiple attacks at different locations, creating confusion for the enemy and making it seem like there are more fighters than there actually are. When the enemy is busy trying to defend multiple places at once, it spreads their forces thin, making them vulnerable.

Guerrilla warfare often uses what is called "psychological warfare." This means that guerrilla fighters try to make the enemy feel afraid, confused, or unsure of their surroundings. One way to do this is by setting up traps or using fake attacks to make the enemy feel like danger is everywhere. For example, guerrilla fighters might set off an explosion in one area to draw the enemy's attention and then attack from another side. By constantly keeping the enemy on edge, they make it difficult for them to feel safe or to know where the next attack might come from. Over time, this can wear down the enemy's spirit and make them less eager to fight.

Guerrilla fighters also depend heavily on support from local communities. Because they often fight against a much larger and better-equipped force, they need help from the people who live in the area. Local villagers might provide food, shelter, or information about enemy movements. This support is crucial because it allows guerrilla fighters to survive in areas where traditional armies might struggle. Local support also means that the guerrilla fighters are not alone in their fight; they have the loyalty and trust of the people, which strengthens their cause and provides a hidden network of assistance that's hard for the enemy to break.

Another important part of guerrilla warfare is avoiding big battles. Unlike traditional armies that try to win through one decisive fight, guerrilla fighters prefer smaller skirmishes that cause damage but don't last long. This helps them avoid heavy losses, as they rarely stay in one place long enough for the enemy to surround them. By engaging in short, sharp attacks and then disappearing, they can gradually weaken the enemy without putting themselves at great risk. This "hit-and-run" style of fighting is one of the trademarks of guerrilla warfare. Each attack might be small, but over time, they add up and can have a big impact on the enemy's strength and morale.

One clever trick used in guerrilla warfare is blending in with the surroundings or with the local population. Guerrilla fighters often dress in ordinary clothes rather than military uniforms, so they look just like regular people. This makes it difficult for the enemy to tell who is a guerrilla fighter and who isn't. Sometimes, the enemy is hesitant to attack because they don't want to hurt innocent people. This camouflage tactic helps guerrilla fighters stay hidden and gives them a significant advantage, as the enemy struggles to identify who they are really fighting.

Guerrilla tactics were famously used by Native American tribes when they defended their land against invading forces. Rather than fighting in open fields, where they would be vulnerable, they used the forests, rivers, and mountains to hide and surprise their enemies. They became experts at using their knowledge of the land to launch quick attacks and then disappear. This way of fighting made it very difficult for larger armies to defeat them because they could not predict where the next attack would come from or where the Native American warriors were hiding.

One of the major goals of guerrilla warfare is to wear down the enemy's will to fight. In a long, drawn-out conflict, even a strong army can become tired, frustrated, and eventually less willing to continue. Guerrilla fighters know that time is often on their side because they are fighting to defend their home, while the invading army is far from home and may not be as determined to stay for a long time. By stretching out the conflict and making it costly and difficult, guerrilla fighters aim to exhaust the enemy and eventually force them to give up and leave.

In modern times, guerrilla warfare continues to be a powerful strategy, especially for smaller groups fighting against bigger, more advanced armies. With new technology, guerrilla fighters have found ways to adapt, using the internet, mobile phones, and other modern tools to communicate and coordinate attacks. They might also use cyber tactics to spread misinformation or gather intelligence on the enemy. While the basic principles of guerrilla warfare remain the same, the tools and methods evolve to match the times, keeping this ancient fighting style relevant even today.

In summary, guerrilla warfare is about fighting smart rather than strong. By using surprise attacks, knowing the land, blending in with the population, disrupting supplies, and moving in small groups, guerrilla fighters have developed a way to stand up to much larger forces. This style of warfare requires bravery, quick thinking, and a strong connection with local people who provide support. Guerrilla warfare shows that even against a more powerful enemy, intelligence, resourcefulness, and determination can make a difference. It's a strategy that has helped many smaller groups defend their freedom and resist stronger forces throughout history, proving that sometimes, the best way to win isn't through strength alone but by using clever tactics and the element of surprise.

Chapter 11: The Power of Alliances

The power of alliances is one of the most important strategies in history, especially in times of conflict and war. An alliance is a partnership or agreement between two or more groups, nations, or people to support each other for a common purpose. When nations or groups form alliances, they join forces, share resources, and stand together to achieve goals they might not be able to reach alone. In battles and wars, alliances can mean the difference between winning and losing because they allow countries or groups to combine their strengths, pool their resources, and support each other in tough times.

Imagine you're playing a team game, and your team isn't as strong or as big as the other team. But if you team up with another group, you'll have more players, more resources, and more ideas to win the game. In history, alliances have worked in a similar way. Countries facing strong enemies have often chosen to form alliances with other countries so that together, they could balance out or even outmatch the enemy's power. The combined strength, resources, and knowledge that alliances bring can be much stronger than what a country could achieve alone.

One famous example of the power of alliances in history is during World War II. At the start of the war, Nazi Germany was very powerful and had already taken over many parts of Europe. But countries like the United Kingdom, the United States, the Soviet Union, and several others came together to form an alliance known as the Allies. The Allies agreed to work together to stop the spread of Nazi Germany and its allies. They coordinated their military strategies, shared intelligence, and provided each other with supplies and support. By standing together, they created a powerful force that was eventually able to overcome Nazi Germany and its allies, leading to the end of the war. This alliance was essential because no single country could have won that war on its own against such a powerful enemy.

Alliances are not only useful in fighting wars but also in preventing them. Sometimes, when countries form alliances, they create something called a balance of power. This balance means that no single country or group of countries becomes too powerful. For example, if one country tries to become too strong and threatens others, the countries in the alliance can come together to prevent that from happening. This balance makes it less likely for anyone to start a war because they know that if they do, they'll have to face multiple countries united against them. This idea of balance through alliances can create a safer and more stable world.

A great example of alliances preventing conflict is the Triple Alliance and Triple Entente before World War I. The Triple Alliance included Germany, Austria-Hungary, and Italy, while the Triple Entente included France, Russia, and the United Kingdom. Although tensions were high in Europe at the time, these alliances created a balance of power. Countries were cautious about starting conflicts because they knew it would lead to a large and dangerous war involving multiple powerful nations. While it didn't prevent World War I forever, it did create a temporary balance that kept major conflicts from breaking out for a time.

Alliances also allow countries to share their unique strengths and resources. One country might be very skilled at building ships, while another has a strong army, and a third has valuable resources like oil or minerals. When they form an alliance, they can share what they're good at with each other. This makes them all stronger and better prepared for challenges. For example, during World War II, the United States had a lot of resources and could produce many weapons, tanks, and airplanes. Meanwhile, the Soviet Union had a very large army. By combining these strengths, the Allies were able to create a powerful fighting force that could take on the Axis powers on different fronts, from Europe to the Pacific.

Another powerful alliance in history was the one formed between the Greek city-states during ancient times. Greece was made up of many independent cities like Athens, Sparta, and Corinth. They each had their own governments and armies and often competed with each other. But when the Persian Empire, one of the biggest and most powerful empires of the time, threatened to conquer Greece, the city-states realized that they would need to put aside their differences and work together. They formed an alliance called the Hellenic League, combining their armies to defend Greece from the Persians. This alliance allowed them to pool their forces and strategies, and they were able to defeat the much larger Persian forces in battles like the famous Battle of Marathon and the Battle of Salamis. By working together, the Greeks were able to protect their land and their way of life from a powerful invader.

Alliances can also create a sense of unity and purpose, bringing together people who might otherwise have little in common. When countries form alliances, they often need to communicate, share ideas, and understand each other better. This helps build friendships between countries and encourages them to support each other not only during wars but also in times of peace. For example, after World War II, many European countries formed an alliance called NATO (North Atlantic Treaty Organization) to protect each other from threats. By working closely together, these countries built strong bonds that went beyond just military support; they started trading with each other, exchanging ideas, and even working together on scientific research and education. This unity has kept these countries close and supportive of each other for decades, showing how alliances can create lasting friendships that go beyond the battlefield.

Alliances don't only happen between countries. In history, different groups within a single country have also formed alliances to reach common goals. For example, during the American Revolutionary War, the American colonists, who wanted independence from British rule, formed an alliance with France. France sent soldiers, ships, and supplies to help the Americans fight the British. This support was crucial because Britain had a powerful navy, and the American colonies didn't have the resources to fight on their own. With the help of their French allies, the Americans were able to win important battles, eventually leading to their independence from Britain. This alliance showed that even though the American colonists and the French had different cultures and languages, they could come together for a shared purpose and achieve something incredible.

Another interesting example of alliances is the Iroquois Confederacy, a powerful alliance of six Native American nations: the Mohawk, Oneida, Onondaga, Cayuga, Seneca, and Tuscarora. These nations joined forces to form a confederacy, which was a type of alliance where they agreed to work together and support each other. This alliance helped them become very powerful in North America, as they could defend themselves against outside threats and resolve disputes among themselves peacefully. The Iroquois Confederacy lasted for hundreds of years and inspired other groups around the world with its model of cooperation, showing that alliances can create peace and stability, not just military power.

Alliances also play an important role in helping people in need. Sometimes, countries form alliances to provide aid and relief to those affected by natural disasters, disease outbreaks, or food shortages. For instance, after a big earthquake or flood, allied countries might send supplies, medical teams, and rescue workers to help. By pooling their resources and expertise, these countries can provide assistance more quickly and effectively than if they acted alone. This type of alliance is based on compassion and a shared sense of responsibility to help others, showing that alliances are not only about war and defense but also about kindness and cooperation.

However, alliances can also be complicated. When countries or groups enter into an alliance, they have to make promises to help each other, even if they don't always agree on everything. This can sometimes lead to difficult situations. For example, if one member of an alliance decides to start a conflict, other members might feel pressured to join in, even if they didn't originally want to fight. This happened in World War I when alliances pulled several countries into the conflict, which made the war much larger and more destructive than it might have been otherwise. Sometimes, being part of an alliance means making tough choices to honor agreements and support allies, even when it's challenging.

In modern times, alliances continue to play a vital role in maintaining peace, security, and cooperation around the world. Organizations like the United Nations and the European Union are examples of alliances formed to address global issues such as climate change, poverty, and health crises. Through these alliances, countries work together to find solutions to problems that affect everyone, regardless of borders. These alliances focus on diplomacy and problem-solving rather than conflict, showing how alliances can create a more united and peaceful world by bringing together diverse nations with a common purpose.

The power of alliances lies in their ability to create strength through unity. By joining forces, countries and groups can achieve goals that would be difficult, if not impossible, to reach alone. Alliances bring together different strengths, ideas, and resources, allowing members to support each other in times of need and to stand stronger against challenges. They teach us that cooperation and mutual support can be as powerful as any weapon, and that by working together, even the biggest obstacles can be overcome. Throughout history, alliances have shaped the course of battles, wars, and even entire nations, proving that the power of alliances is a force that can change the world.

Chapter 12: Siege Warfare Techniques

Siege warfare was a type of battle technique used in ancient and medieval times when armies wanted to capture a well-defended city, fortress, or castle. When a city or castle had thick walls, towers, and was guarded by soldiers, it was almost impossible for attackers to get inside without a long and careful plan. Sieges were battles that could last weeks, months, or even years, because they involved trying to weaken the defenders inside until they had no choice but to surrender. During a siege, attackers would surround the place they wanted to conquer, cutting off supplies like food and water to weaken the defenders. Meanwhile, they would use a variety of creative and powerful techniques to try to break down the walls, sneak inside, or force the defenders to give up.

One of the main techniques in siege warfare was called "starving out" the defenders. By surrounding the castle or city, the attackers made sure that no one could enter or leave. This meant that the people inside couldn't bring in fresh supplies of food, water, or medical items. Over time, the people inside the walls would begin to run out of resources, especially food. Hunger would set in, and people would grow weaker, making it difficult for soldiers to stay strong enough to defend their walls. Sometimes, the attackers would even poison nearby rivers or wells to cut off the defenders' water supply. This tactic was slow, but it often worked because people inside would get desperate, and eventually, they might open the gates and surrender.

Another siege technique involved building large siege towers. These were huge wooden towers that attackers would construct outside the walls. They were made tall enough to reach the top of the city walls so that soldiers inside the tower could cross over and attack the defenders. Soldiers would hide inside these towers as they were slowly moved closer to the wall. Some siege towers even had wheels so they could be pushed forward. The towers protected the attackers from arrows and stones thrown by the defenders. Once the tower was close enough to the wall, a bridge would lower, and the soldiers would storm across it to try to capture the wall from the defenders. Defenders would sometimes try to set the towers on fire with flaming arrows to stop them from reaching the walls, which is why many siege towers were covered in animal skins soaked in water to make them harder to burn.

Catapults and trebuchets were powerful weapons used in sieges to break down walls or create chaos inside the city. A catapult was a machine that could fling large stones, fireballs, or other heavy objects at the walls or even inside the city. The goal was to damage the walls or to create fear and confusion among the people inside. The trebuchet was similar to a catapult but even more powerful and accurate. It used a long arm and a heavy counterweight to hurl huge stones, sometimes weighing as much as a small car, over great distances. When these stones hit the walls, they could cause serious cracks or even collapse sections of the wall. Some attackers also used these machines to throw burning materials or even diseased animal carcasses into the city, hoping to spread illness and fear among the defenders.

Another dangerous tactic was tunneling, also called "mining." Attackers would dig tunnels underneath the walls of the fortress or city they were trying to capture. These tunnels were carefully dug and supported by wooden beams so that they wouldn't collapse. The goal was to dig under the wall until they reached a point where they could weaken its foundation. Once the tunnel was in the right place, the attackers would fill it with flammable materials like dry wood or straw and set it on fire. The fire would burn the wooden supports, causing the tunnel to collapse, and the wall above would often crumble as well. This technique was very risky because the tunnel could cave in, trapping or injuring the miners. To defend against tunneling, the people inside the city would sometimes dig counter-tunnels, hoping to find and stop the attackers underground before they could cause damage.

Battering rams were another important tool in siege warfare. These were long, heavy logs, often with a metal tip, that soldiers would swing back and forth to slam into the gates of a fortress or city. The repeated blows would weaken the gate until it eventually broke down, allowing attackers to rush in. Some battering rams were very simple, just a big log carried by several men, but others were more advanced. Some had a roof to protect the soldiers from arrows or hot oil poured down by the defenders. Breaking through the gate was always one of the most dangerous parts of a siege, as it meant coming face-to-face with the defenders who were waiting just on the other side.

Defenders, of course, had their own techniques to fight back against siege attacks. One common defense was to pour boiling oil or hot sand down on attackers who got too close to the walls. Defenders might also drop large stones on siege towers or battering rams to crush them and stop their progress. Another defensive technique was to build double walls with space in between. If the attackers managed to break through the first wall, they would find themselves in a trapped area with the second wall in front of them, allowing defenders to attack from both sides. This made it even harder for attackers to reach the main parts of the city or castle.

Moats were another popular defense against sieges. A moat is a deep, wide ditch, usually filled with water, that surrounds a castle or fortress. Moats made it very difficult for attackers to get close to the walls because they would need to find a way across. Some attackers tried building makeshift bridges, but defenders could often destroy these bridges or set them on fire. Some moats were filled with sharp stakes hidden underwater to injure anyone trying to swim across. Moats also made tunneling much harder because the water could flood any tunnel dug underneath it, stopping the attackers' progress.

Sometimes, if the attackers had to wait a long time during a siege, they would build temporary camps and even small villages around the city. This is called a siege camp. They would set up tents for soldiers to sleep in and kitchens to prepare food. The camps would be surrounded by their own defenses, like trenches or wooden walls, to protect against surprise attacks from the defenders or any other armies trying to come to the city's rescue. These camps helped the attackers stay close to the city for long periods, but they were also dangerous because the defenders could try to launch sudden attacks on the camps to disrupt the siege.

During a siege, attackers sometimes tried to use psychological tactics to scare the defenders into surrendering. One tactic was to make it seem like their army was much larger than it actually was. They might spread out their soldiers in a way that made it look like they had more men, or they might light extra campfires at night so the defenders would see many lights and think there was a huge army outside. Sometimes, attackers would send messengers to shout threats or promises of mercy if the defenders surrendered quickly. Psychological tactics were used to weaken the morale of those inside the city, making them feel hopeless or afraid, and sometimes this was enough to make them surrender without much fighting.

Siege warfare also led to the invention of some clever and unusual weapons. One was the Greek fire, a mysterious and powerful liquid that could burn even on water. The Byzantine Empire famously used Greek fire to defend their cities and ships from attackers. When attackers got close, defenders would throw or spray Greek fire at them, creating walls of flame that were nearly impossible to put out. Another unique weapon was the scorpion, a kind of giant crossbow that could shoot arrows or bolts at the attackers from a great distance. Defenders would use scorpions to hit soldiers in siege towers or at the base of the wall, slowing their progress.

As technology advanced, siege warfare became even more intense. Gunpowder and cannons changed the way sieges were fought. Cannons were powerful enough to smash through walls that would have been nearly impossible to breach with older weapons like battering rams. With cannons, attackers could cause massive destruction in a short amount of time, making sieges even more deadly. Defenders had to build thicker walls or create angled walls that could better withstand cannon fire. The use of cannons in siege warfare marked a new era, where fortresses had to adapt to these powerful new weapons.

Although sieges were often brutal and could take a long time, they were sometimes the only way for armies to take over well-defended places. The strategy behind siege warfare required patience, planning, and a good understanding of both offense and defense. Commanders needed to think carefully about how to position their forces, where to build their siege engines, and how to keep their own soldiers supplied during long waits. For defenders, sieges were a test of endurance, bravery, and resilience. They had to find ways to hold out against hunger, fear, and constant attacks, hoping that help would arrive or that the attackers would give up.

In many cases, the outcome of a siege could decide the fate of an entire region or country. If a city was captured, it could open up the surrounding area to invasion, allowing the attackers to move in and take control. However, if the defenders managed to hold out and win the siege, it could strengthen their position and make it harder for future attackers to challenge them. Over time, siege warfare helped shape the rise and fall of kingdoms and empires, and the techniques and lessons learned from these long, grueling battles continued to influence military strategies for centuries.

In the end, siege warfare was a challenging and complicated form of battle that showed the incredible creativity and determination of both attackers and defenders. It required a mix of strength, strategy, and resilience to succeed, and those who could master it held great power. Though brutal, siege warfare played a huge role in history, teaching people how to adapt, invent new technologies, and stand strong under pressure. Each siege was like a high-stakes game of patience and strategy, where both sides fought hard to outlast the other, sometimes leading to the rise of heroes and legends that are still remembered today.

Chapter 13: Night Raids and Stealth Moves

Night raids and stealth moves have been powerful and daring strategies used throughout history. These tactics involve surprising the enemy under the cover of darkness or using sneaky, quiet moves to avoid being seen. In battles and wars, night raids and stealthy approaches were often used by armies or smaller groups who wanted to attack without being noticed or who needed to make a big impact without a huge number of soldiers. These tactics are not only exciting but also very clever because they require planning, patience, and bravery. When done well, night raids and stealth moves could turn the tide of a battle, give weaker forces a fighting chance, and even help win wars.

Nighttime offered a huge advantage for attackers who wanted to stay hidden because it made it much harder for defenders to see them coming. In the dark, armies could move more quietly and get closer to enemy camps without being noticed. Defenders were also often tired at night, which made them less alert. Many soldiers might be asleep, and the guards on duty could be worn out after a long day, making them more likely to miss sounds or movements. This is why night raids were often very effective — they caught the enemy off guard when they were at their most vulnerable. Attacking at night also made it easier for smaller groups of soldiers to take on a larger enemy force because they could surprise them and cause chaos before the defenders even knew what was happening.

One of the earliest recorded examples of a night raid was in ancient Greece during the Trojan War. The Greeks wanted to capture the city of Troy but couldn't break through its strong walls even after years of trying. Finally, they came up with a clever stealth plan involving the famous Trojan Horse. The Greeks pretended to leave, leaving behind a giant wooden horse as a "gift." However, hidden inside the horse were Greek soldiers. The Trojans brought the horse inside their city walls, thinking it was a victory prize. At night, when the city was quiet and the Trojans were asleep, the soldiers climbed out of the horse, opened the gates for the rest of the Greek army, and took over the city. Although it wasn't exactly a night raid, it showed how important surprise and stealth could be in battle.

One of the most famous night raids in history happened during the American Revolutionary War. General George Washington led his troops across the icy Delaware River on Christmas night in 1776. The American soldiers were cold, tired, and in desperate need of a victory. They knew that the British troops, along with their German allies called the Hessians, were stationed across the river in Trenton, New Jersey. Washington decided to surprise the Hessians with a nighttime crossing and an early morning attack. The Hessians weren't expecting an attack on Christmas, so they weren't prepared. Washington's troops stormed into Trenton and caught the Hessians off guard, winning a much-needed victory for the American forces. This night raid became legendary and is still remembered today as a clever use of stealth, timing, and surprise.

In ancient China, night raids were also a common tactic. Sun Tzu, the famous military strategist who wrote *The Art of War*, often emphasized the importance of using surprise and deception in battles. According to Sun Tzu, if you knew your enemy well and chose the right moment, you could defeat them even if they were stronger or had more soldiers. One way to do this was through night raids. By attacking at night, an army could take advantage of the darkness to move swiftly and confuse the enemy. The element of surprise was so powerful that it could make up for any disadvantages in numbers or strength. Sun Tzu's ideas about using the night and stealth in battle influenced not only the Chinese but also military leaders around the world for centuries.

Stealth moves weren't always about direct attacks, though. Sometimes, armies would sneak close to the enemy to gather information. In Japan, ninja warriors were famous for their stealth skills. They were masters of moving quietly, hiding in the shadows, and avoiding detection. Ninjas were often hired to sneak into enemy camps or castles to find out their plans, steal important documents, or listen in on secret conversations. They wore dark clothing to blend into the night and used special tools to help them climb walls or escape quickly. Ninja tactics were all about avoiding fights unless necessary. Their goal was to complete their mission without being seen, showing that stealth moves could be just as effective for gathering information as for launching attacks.

During the Middle Ages, knights and soldiers often used night raids to try to capture enemy castles. Castles were difficult to attack because they had high walls, guards, and usually a moat or other obstacles. Trying to break through a castle's defenses during the day was almost impossible, so attackers would sometimes try to sneak in at night. In some cases, soldiers might swim across a moat under cover of darkness, then climb the castle walls with ropes or ladders. Once inside, they would quietly take out the guards and open the gates for the rest of the army to enter. These raids were dangerous because if the attackers were caught, they would have to fight without much support, but if successful, they could take over a powerful fortress without a long siege.

Another famous example of a stealth move is the Doolittle Raid during World War II. This raid was a surprise air attack on Japan by the United States after the attack on Pearl Harbor. American pilots, led by Lieutenant Colonel James Doolittle, flew their planes close to Japan without being detected. Although they launched the attack during the day, the whole mission was a stealth operation because the pilots had to fly under the radar and avoid Japanese defenses. The goal wasn't to cause huge damage but to show Japan that the U.S. could strike back. The raid boosted American morale and surprised the Japanese, who hadn't expected an attack so close to home.

One of the most challenging parts of night raids and stealth operations was communication. Because it was dark and soldiers had to be quiet, they often couldn't use loud commands or signals. In ancient times, soldiers sometimes used hand signals or whispered messages to communicate during night raids. Later, they developed more advanced techniques like using signals from lanterns, torches, or even animal sounds. For example, one soldier might make the sound of an owl to signal others to move forward or a whistle to signal retreat. These communication methods had to be simple yet effective because one wrong move could ruin the whole operation.

The use of camouflage was another important part of stealth moves. During a night raid, soldiers might cover themselves in dark clothing or mud to blend into the environment and avoid being seen. In World War II, soldiers even wore special clothing designed to blend into forests, snowy areas, or other landscapes, helping them move quietly through enemy territory without being noticed. Camouflage and stealth often went hand in hand because the ability to blend in was essential to getting close to the enemy without drawing attention.

In modern times, night raids and stealth tactics have become even more advanced with technology. Special forces like the Navy SEALs in the United States are trained to carry out night raids with incredible precision. They use night-vision goggles, which allow them to see in the dark, giving them an advantage over the enemy. They also use silencers on their weapons so they can move and attack quietly. Helicopters can drop soldiers into enemy areas quickly and silently, allowing them to strike and then retreat before the enemy even knows they're there. Modern night raids rely on a mix of high-tech equipment and careful planning, showing how these ancient tactics have been adapted for the present day.

Night raids and stealth moves required incredible bravery and trust among soldiers. Each person had to move carefully and quietly, relying on the others to do the same. A single noise could alert the enemy, ruining the surprise and putting everyone in danger. These tactics weren't for everyone; they required soldiers who were calm under pressure, could move quickly and quietly, and knew how to follow instructions without hesitation. The success of a night raid often depended on each soldier doing their part perfectly, without making any mistakes.

In conclusion, night raids and stealth moves have been valuable tactics throughout history, allowing smaller forces to take on bigger enemies, gather intelligence, or strike at the heart of enemy territory without detection. These tactics took advantage of the cover of darkness, the element of surprise, and the use of quiet movements to create confusion and fear among defenders. While night raids and stealth moves were risky, they often made a huge difference in battles and wars. They show how creativity, bravery, and careful planning can sometimes be even more powerful than sheer numbers or strength. From ancient Greece to modern special forces, the art of moving unseen and striking at the right moment continues to be an important part of military strategy.

Chapter 14: Sea Battles and Naval Strategy

Sea battles and naval strategies have been an important part of warfare for thousands of years, allowing armies and empires to control trade routes, protect coastlines, and conquer new lands. Battles fought on water have always been different from those on land, requiring special ships, unique weapons, and clever tactics to navigate the challenges of open seas, unpredictable winds, and powerful waves. Commanders had to understand not only the power of their own ships but also how to use the sea itself as a weapon, taking advantage of currents, tides, and even weather to surprise their enemies. Naval battles changed the way wars were fought, with entire nations rising to power through their ability to command the seas.

In ancient times, ships were often powered by oars, with soldiers and sailors rowing in rhythm to propel their vessels forward. These early warships, like the Greek triremes and the Roman quinqueremes, had multiple rows of oars on each side, allowing them to move quickly through the water. The main tactic in ancient sea battles was ramming. Ships were built with strong, pointed hulls that could smash into the sides of enemy ships, causing them to sink. The goal was to maneuver one's ship close enough to ram the enemy, then back away and let the water do the rest. In the narrow waters around Greece and the Mediterranean, this tactic worked well because commanders could use tight formations and quickly maneuver their ships into attacking positions.

The Battle of Salamis in 480 BCE is one of the most famous sea battles from ancient times. The Greeks were facing a much larger Persian fleet led by King Xerxes. Knowing they couldn't defeat the Persian navy in a straight fight, the Greeks lured the Persian ships into a narrow strait where it was difficult for them to move freely. In the tight space, the Greek triremes, which were smaller and faster, were able to ram the Persian ships, sinking many of them and causing chaos among the Persian fleet. This battle showed the importance of strategy and choosing the right location for a fight. Even though the Greeks had fewer ships, they won by using the geography of the sea to their advantage.

As naval warfare developed, so did the ships and tactics. The Vikings, who sailed across the seas in the Middle Ages, used longships that were fast, lightweight, and able to sail in both open seas and shallow rivers. Viking longships had shallow hulls, which allowed them to travel close to shore and even sail upriver, where other ships couldn't reach. This gave the Vikings the ability to launch surprise raids on coastal towns and then retreat quickly before enemies could organize a defense. The Vikings were skilled sailors who knew how to read the stars, wind patterns, and ocean currents, allowing them to navigate over long distances. Their strategy combined speed, surprise, and superior knowledge of the seas, making them a feared naval power in Europe.

In the Age of Exploration, ships evolved to become larger and more powerful, as European nations like Spain, Portugal, and England began exploring and colonizing distant lands. These nations built fleets of ships that could carry large amounts of cargo and had powerful cannons mounted along the sides. In the 16th and 17th centuries, naval battles began to rely more on artillery than on ramming or boarding. Ships would line up side by side in formations known as "lines of battle," firing their cannons in powerful broadsides. This tactic required precise positioning because the ships had to be close enough to hit their targets but far enough to avoid being hit themselves. Commanders had to understand the range and power of their cannons and the speed of their ships, using careful planning to position their fleets in the best possible way.

One of the most famous sea battles of this period was the defeat of the Spanish Armada in 1588. Spain sent a large fleet of ships to invade

England, but the English navy, under commanders like Sir Francis Drake, used smaller, more maneuverable ships to outsmart the Spanish. The English ships could turn and move quickly, firing their cannons and then retreating before the Spanish could respond. Bad weather also played a role in the Spanish Armada's defeat, showing how unpredictable the sea could be. This battle marked a turning point in naval warfare, as it showed that smaller, faster ships with powerful cannons could defeat a larger fleet if they used the right strategy.

During the 18th and 19th centuries, naval strategy became even more complex as ships continued to grow in size and firepower. The use of line formations became standard, with fleets organizing their ships in long lines to maximize their firepower. This tactic was called the "line of battle," where ships would sail in a single line, each one following the next, so they could fire all their cannons at once in powerful, coordinated volleys. The Battle of Trafalgar in 1805 is one of the best examples of this strategy. Admiral Horatio Nelson of the British navy used an innovative approach to break through the French and Spanish lines, dividing their fleet and making it easier to attack each ship separately. Nelson's tactics helped the British win a decisive victory, which secured Britain's dominance over the seas for many years.

One of the most important changes in naval strategy came with the invention of steam-powered ships in the 19th century. Unlike sailing ships, which relied on the wind to move, steamships had engines that allowed them to travel in any direction regardless of wind conditions. This made naval strategy more flexible, as commanders no longer had to worry about the wind. They could position their ships more precisely and make faster, more reliable movements. Steamships also had stronger hulls made of iron, making them tougher and able to withstand more damage. As technology improved, ships were equipped with even more powerful cannons and new weapons like torpedoes, changing the way sea battles were fought once again.

The development of submarines in the early 20th century added a new dimension to naval warfare. Submarines could travel underwater, making them invisible to enemies on the surface. They could sneak up on enemy ships and launch torpedoes without being seen, making them a very dangerous weapon. In both World Wars, submarines were used to great effect. German U-boats, for example, attacked Allied supply ships crossing the Atlantic Ocean, trying to cut off essential supplies from reaching Europe. This type of warfare was known as "unrestricted submarine warfare" and forced navies to develop new strategies for protecting their ships, such as traveling in groups called convoys and using sonar to detect submarines.

Aircraft carriers became the dominant force in naval strategy during World War II. These massive ships could carry dozens of airplanes, allowing them to strike targets far away. Instead of ships fighting each other directly, aircraft from carriers would take off, attack enemy ships or bases, and then return to the carrier. This allowed naval forces to reach far beyond the range of traditional ships, changing the nature of sea battles. The Battle of Midway in 1942 was a turning point in the Pacific theater of World War II, where American aircraft carriers ambushed a Japanese fleet. The planes from the carriers destroyed much of the Japanese fleet, marking the beginning of the end of Japan's dominance in the Pacific. Aircraft carriers showed how air power could extend the reach of a navy, making them essential to modern naval strategy.

Naval strategy also includes controlling important waterways and chokepoints, like straits and canals, which are narrow areas where ships must pass through. By controlling these areas, a navy can block enemy ships from reaching certain places or force them to take longer routes. For example, the Strait of Gibraltar is a narrow passage that connects the Atlantic Ocean to the Mediterranean Sea. Whoever controls Gibraltar can control the movement of ships between these two important bodies of water. During wartime, navies often tried to capture or defend these strategic points to protect their own ships and block enemy movement.

Modern naval strategy is a combination of many of these tactics, with new technology making ships faster, stronger, and more versatile. Battleships have largely been replaced by smaller, more advanced ships like destroyers and frigates, which can move quickly and carry a variety of weapons. Modern navies also use stealth technology to make their ships harder to detect, making it easier to move undetected. Submarines, aircraft carriers, and advanced missile systems play a huge role, giving navies the ability to strike from great distances and stay hidden from enemy forces.

Sea battles and naval strategy have always been about more than just the ships themselves. They require careful planning, a deep understanding of the sea, and the ability to adapt to changing conditions. Commanders need to think about how to use wind, weather, and currents to their advantage, as well as how to position their ships in a way that maximizes their strengths and protects their weaknesses. Over the centuries, the tools and tactics of naval warfare have changed, but the core strategies — surprise, speed, positioning, and control of the sea — remain essential.

Naval power continues to be a crucial factor in global politics. Countries with strong navies can protect their coastlines, keep trade routes open, and project power across the world. In times of conflict, a powerful navy can block supplies, defend allies, and deter potential enemies. With modern ships equipped with missiles, radar, and sophisticated defense systems, navies are more powerful and complex than ever, making them an essential part of any nation's defense strategy. As technology advances, sea battles and naval strategy will keep evolving, but the courage, skill, and strategy needed to command the seas will always remain at the heart of naval warfare.

Chapter 15: The Role of Psychological Warfare

Psychological warfare is a strategy in which armies and leaders try to affect the minds and emotions of their enemies instead of just fighting with weapons. The goal is to weaken the enemy's morale, make them doubt their chances of winning, or create confusion and fear so they might give up, retreat, or surrender without even needing to engage in a direct battle. This type of warfare can be as powerful as physical attacks because it targets the thoughts, feelings, and decisions of an enemy, which can change the course of a conflict. Psychological tactics have been used throughout history, with leaders and armies using clever tricks, intimidating displays, and messages to weaken the enemy's will to fight. Winning a battle in the mind often means that a leader doesn't need to risk as many soldiers or resources, which can make psychological warfare a very effective strategy.

One of the oldest forms of psychological warfare is intimidation. Ancient armies often tried to appear much larger or stronger than they actually were to scare their opponents. For example, when the Greek soldier Alexander the Great led his army to battle, he sometimes made his soldiers shout loudly and beat their shields as they marched. This noise made the Greek army sound massive and powerful, even if they were outnumbered, which intimidated their enemies. Alexander also wore a shining, golden helmet and rode a large horse that made him stand out. His impressive appearance made his enemies feel like they were up against a powerful and almost unstoppable force. Many enemies feared him so much that they surrendered without fighting because they believed they couldn't win against such a determined and strong leader.

Another famous example of psychological warfare was used by Genghis Khan, the leader of the Mongol Empire. The Mongols were known for their fierce, disciplined warriors and their fast, skilled horsemen. Genghis Khan used his army's fearsome reputation to frighten entire cities into surrendering before he even attacked. One of his tactics was to send messengers to a city with a warning, offering the people a chance to surrender peacefully. If they didn't, he would promise destruction and devastation. The Mongols were known for being merciless when they captured cities that resisted, so many towns and cities surrendered without a fight to avoid the wrath of the Mongol army. By spreading stories of their strength and ruthlessness, Genghis Khan didn't always need to battle for each city; sometimes, just the thought of fighting him was terrifying enough to make people give up.

Psychological warfare also involves deception, which means tricking the enemy into making mistakes. In ancient China, Sun Tzu, the author of *The Art of War*, wrote about the importance of deceiving the enemy to gain an advantage. He believed that if an enemy could be tricked into thinking the wrong thing, it would be easier to defeat them. One example of this was the use of fake retreats. An army would pretend to be losing and start to retreat, making the enemy believe they were winning. As the enemy chased them, thinking they were about to achieve victory, they would be led into a trap, surrounded, and defeated. By playing with the enemy's expectations and tricking them into a false sense of confidence, commanders could turn a seemingly losing situation into a victory.

In the American Civil War, psychological warfare was also used by generals on both sides. General William Tecumseh Sherman of the Union Army used a tactic called "total war" to weaken the Confederate states' will to fight. During his famous "March to the Sea," he led his troops through Georgia, destroying farms, railways, and factories, and burning down supplies that could be useful to the Confederate army. By doing this, he didn't just destroy resources; he created fear and despair among the Confederate civilians and soldiers, who saw their homes and livelihoods ruined. Sherman's goal was to make the

Southern people feel so hopeless and weary of war that they would pressure their leaders to surrender. His tactics may have seemed harsh, but they were effective in ending the war sooner and preventing further battles.

Propaganda is another key tool in psychological warfare. Propaganda involves spreading information, whether true or false, to influence people's opinions and beliefs. During World War II, propaganda was used by both the Allies and the Axis powers to try to influence each other's soldiers and citizens. The Germans, under the direction of Adolf Hitler, produced a lot of propaganda aimed at making their army seem unbeatable, to boost their own morale while intimidating their enemies. The British and Americans, meanwhile, created leaflets and radio broadcasts to encourage German soldiers to surrender, telling them that their defeat was inevitable and that their leaders were leading them into disaster. Leaflets would be dropped from planes over enemy lines, with messages designed to make soldiers question their leaders, their cause, or the strength of their own forces.

Even in modern times, psychological warfare is used to make enemy leaders and soldiers feel uncertain or fearful. For example, during the Gulf War in the early 1990s, the United States used broadcasts and leaflets to encourage Iraqi soldiers to surrender, warning them of the powerful forces against them and urging them to save their own lives. The leaflets promised fair treatment if they surrendered and painted a grim picture of what would happen if they continued to fight. The goal was to make the soldiers doubt their chances and make it easier for the U.S. to achieve victory without risking as many lives.

The display of overwhelming strength is another way psychological warfare works. Some countries hold massive military parades to show off their soldiers, tanks, planes, and missiles. These displays are meant to show potential enemies the power and discipline of their armed forces, making them think twice before considering any acts of aggression. Sometimes, nations even conduct military exercises close to the borders of other countries as a reminder of their strength and readiness to defend themselves. This approach is meant to send a warning without actually starting a battle, relying on the idea that fear and respect can prevent conflict.

Psychological warfare can even involve attacking the symbols or leaders of an enemy. When an important leader is defeated or captured, it can greatly weaken the morale of the enemy army. For example, during the Napoleonic Wars, Napoleon Bonaparte inspired his soldiers with his charisma and leadership. He was loved by his troops, and his presence gave them courage. When Napoleon was finally defeated and exiled, his soldiers felt the loss deeply. Without him, they were less motivated and lost their fighting spirit. Similarly, when a flag or symbol of a country is captured, it can cause despair among the soldiers, who see it as a sign that they are losing. Armies know how important symbols and leaders are to morale, so they sometimes target them to shake the enemy's confidence.

In some cases, psychological warfare involves creating confusion or making the enemy doubt their own information. A modern example is the use of "fake news" or disinformation, where one side spreads false information to mislead or confuse the other side. For example, spreading a rumor about an upcoming attack can force the enemy to move troops to a certain location, only to find out that the attack was never planned. By confusing the enemy, commanders can force them to waste resources and time, making them weaker when the real battle begins.

Psychological warfare requires a deep understanding of human emotions, thoughts, and reactions. The most successful commanders in history knew how to inspire confidence in their own soldiers while weakening the morale of the enemy. It's a game of strategy that involves predicting how people will react to fear, uncertainty, or even hope. Sometimes, this means using tricks and deception, other times, it's about showing strength or spreading information that makes the enemy doubt themselves.

The effects of psychological warfare can last long after a battle or war is over. Soldiers and civilians who have been affected by it might feel shaken or uncertain about their own beliefs. This type of warfare can be powerful because it doesn't rely on physical strength alone but targets something just as important: the human mind.

Chapter 16: Using Nature as an Ally

Using nature as an ally in warfare has been an important tactic for armies and leaders throughout history. Nature provides landscapes, weather, and resources that can help one side gain an advantage over another, turning the environment into a powerful tool in battle. Commanders who understood how to use the natural world to their benefit could make their armies stronger and even outsmart enemies who weren't prepared for the challenges that nature could create. Using mountains, rivers, forests, and deserts as part of a strategy allowed armies to hide, surprise their enemies, protect themselves, or make it difficult for enemies to advance. Learning to use nature as an ally takes skill, patience, and a deep understanding of the land, but it can lead to victories that might seem impossible otherwise.

One of the earliest and most famous examples of using nature in warfare was Hannibal's journey through the Alps in 218 BCE during the Second Punic War. Hannibal, a Carthaginian general, wanted to attack Rome by crossing the Alps, which were tall, snowy mountains that separated Italy from the rest of Europe. The Romans did not expect an enemy to cross the Alps because it was a very dangerous journey, especially for an army with elephants, horses, and supplies. The freezing temperatures, rocky paths, and steep cliffs were dangerous for soldiers and animals alike. However, Hannibal believed that if he could cross these mountains, he would surprise the Romans, who wouldn't be prepared for an attack from that direction. The journey was incredibly hard, and Hannibal lost many soldiers and animals along the way due to cold and hunger. But by using the natural barrier of the mountains, he was able to catch the Romans off guard and attack from the north, a move that became one of the most daring strategies in history. Hannibal's march through the Alps showed how the environment, even when it's difficult to cross, can be used as a secret pathway for an army willing to take on the challenge.

In ancient China, armies often used rivers as a way to slow down or stop their enemies. Rivers are natural obstacles that can be hard to cross, especially if the water is deep or moving quickly. Armies would sometimes destroy bridges or set up defenses along riverbanks to make it difficult for enemies to cross. Rivers could also act as natural borders, giving one side an advantage in defending their territory. During the Three Kingdoms period in China, the Battle of Red Cliffs was a famous battle where water played a crucial role. The warlord Cao Cao led a large army and navy down the Yangtze River, hoping to conquer his enemies, but his opponents, Sun Quan and Liu Bei, used the river to trap and defeat him. They set Cao Cao's ships on fire, and because his fleet was close together, the flames spread quickly. The river helped trap his ships and allowed Sun Quan and Liu Bei's forces to win, even though they had fewer soldiers. This battle showed how water can be a powerful ally when used wisely, giving smaller forces a chance to defeat a larger army.

Forests have also been used as valuable allies in warfare. Thick forests provide cover and hiding places where armies can wait to ambush their enemies. Soldiers can hide in the trees and strike suddenly, catching the enemy off guard. During the American Revolution, colonists used forests to launch surprise attacks against the British army. The British soldiers were used to open-field battles in Europe, where armies lined up and faced each other directly. However, in the dense forests of America, the colonists used a style of fighting called guerrilla warfare. They hid behind trees and rocks, firing at the British from unexpected places and then disappearing back into the woods. This made it very hard for the British to fight back because they couldn't see their enemies or predict where the next attack would come from. The colonists' knowledge of the land helped them use the forests as an ally, giving them an advantage in battles against a more powerful and better-equipped British army.

Deserts are another type of natural landscape that can be turned into an ally in warfare. Deserts are hot, dry, and often lack water, making them difficult places for armies to march through. In the North African campaigns of World War II, both the Allies and the Axis powers had to learn how to fight in the desert. The extreme heat and sandstorms made it hard for soldiers to see and move, and water was scarce, making it challenging to keep troops hydrated. Desert conditions required special equipment and tactics, as tanks and trucks could get stuck in the sand. However, armies that understood how to navigate the desert and conserve resources could gain an edge over those who were unprepared for the harsh environment. The British forces, led by General Bernard Montgomery, eventually learned how to use the desert to their advantage, outmaneuvering the German Afrika Korps and securing a victory. The harshness of the desert became a tool, making it difficult for the enemy to survive and fight effectively.

Mountains are natural barriers that can serve as protective fortresses for armies. In the rugged terrain of Afghanistan, for example, Afghan fighters have used the mountains to defend against foreign invaders for centuries. The steep, rocky landscape of the mountains made it hard for enemies to advance, giving the defenders a high ground advantage. During the Soviet-Afghan War in the 1980s, Afghan fighters known as the Mujahideen used the mountains to hide and launch surprise attacks against the Soviet forces. They knew the mountain paths and could easily disappear after attacking, making it hard for the Soviets to track them down. By knowing the land better than their enemies, the Afghan fighters used the mountains as a natural fortress, helping them resist a powerful, well-equipped army.

Weather is also a major factor in using nature as an ally. In 1812, Napoleon Bonaparte, the French emperor, invaded Russia with a large army. He expected a quick victory, but the harsh Russian winter became his biggest enemy. As Napoleon's army marched toward Moscow, the weather turned bitterly cold, with temperatures dropping far below freezing. The soldiers were not prepared for such extreme cold, and many of them became sick or froze to death. Snow and ice made it difficult to find food, and the soldiers' thin clothing couldn't protect them from the freezing temperatures. By the time Napoleon's army retreated, it had lost tens of thousands of men to the cold. The Russian winter, combined with the Russians' strategy of burning their own villages and supplies to deny Napoleon's army any resources, turned nature into a powerful ally for Russia, leading to one of Napoleon's greatest defeats.

Another interesting example of using nature involves animals. Horses have been a crucial part of warfare for centuries, providing soldiers with speed and mobility on the battlefield. But other animals, like elephants and even pigeons, have also been used in warfare. In ancient India, war elephants were used to charge at enemy lines, frightening soldiers and causing chaos. These massive animals could trample enemies and break through formations, making them valuable allies. Pigeons were used to carry messages across battlefields, especially during World War I and World War II. Since pigeons could fly over enemy lines, they were able to deliver important messages when other forms of communication were too dangerous or unreliable. Dogs were also trained to carry supplies, find wounded soldiers, or even detect enemy positions. These animals became allies on the battlefield, using their unique abilities to help soldiers.

One of the most powerful ways to use nature as an ally is by knowing how to survive in difficult conditions. In some cases, armies have used plants and trees to provide food and shelter. In the jungles of Southeast Asia, soldiers learned how to find edible plants, make shelters from leaves, and use the jungle to hide from enemies. During the Vietnam War, Vietnamese fighters known as the Viet Cong used the dense jungles to hide from American forces. They built complex tunnel systems underground, which allowed them to move unseen, store supplies, and even set traps for enemy soldiers. The American soldiers struggled to find and fight the Viet Cong in the jungle because they were unfamiliar with the environment. The Viet Cong's knowledge of the jungle gave them a powerful advantage, allowing them to turn nature into a hiding place and a source of supplies.

Rivers and seas can also be used as barriers or pathways. During World War II, the Allies used the English Channel as a natural barrier to protect Britain from German invasion. The channel's rough waters and strong tides made it hard for the Germans to cross, and British forces used their navy to patrol and defend it. Later, when the Allies wanted to invade France, they used the same waters to transport troops across the channel in a massive surprise attack on D-Day. By understanding the tides, weather, and best routes across the water, the Allies were able to use the sea to their advantage and launch one of the largest amphibious assaults in history, which played a major role in winning the war.

Nature can also provide hidden dangers. Swamps, for instance, are full of mud and thick vegetation, which can make movement nearly impossible. Armies that don't know how to navigate swamps can get trapped, making them easy targets. During the American Civil War, some battles were fought in swampy areas where soldiers had to deal with deep mud, bugs, and thick plants that slowed them down and made it hard to fight. However, soldiers who knew how to move through the swamps could use them as hiding places or as ways to escape, outsmarting the enemy by disappearing into the thick, muddy landscape.

Throughout history, armies and leaders who understood how to use nature as an ally often had the upper hand in battle. The natural world can be as powerful as any weapon, offering hidden paths, defensive barriers, and even a way to wear down an enemy without direct combat. From freezing winters to burning deserts, from rushing rivers to towering mountains, nature can either help or harm those who march through it. Leaders who learn to respect and understand nature's strengths and challenges can find ways to use it to their advantage, making it a silent but mighty partner in the art of war.

Chapter 17: Heroic Last Stands

Heroic last stands are legendary moments in history where small groups of brave soldiers face overwhelming odds, knowing they have little chance of survival but choosing to fight anyway. These moments are called "last stands" because the defenders stand their ground, refusing to surrender, even if it means giving their lives. Although they often lose the battle, their courage, determination, and loyalty inspire future generations and leave a lasting impact on history. Heroic last stands teach us about the power of bravery, the bond between comrades, and the importance of standing up for what one believes in, even when the situation seems hopeless. These moments are remembered not just for the outcome but for the strength of spirit shown by those who took part.

One of the most famous last stands in history happened in 480 BCE at the Battle of Thermopylae in ancient Greece. The Persian Empire, led by King Xerxes, wanted to conquer Greece, and he brought a huge army of thousands to do so. To stop the invasion, King Leonidas of Sparta and a small group of Greek soldiers, including 300 Spartans, stood at a narrow pass in the mountains called Thermopylae. The Greeks knew they were vastly outnumbered, but they also knew that if they could hold the pass for as long as possible, it would give the rest of Greece time to prepare. The Spartans and their allies fought bravely, using the narrow pass to their advantage, which limited how many Persian soldiers could attack at once. Despite their smaller numbers, the Greeks held off the Persians for three days. Unfortunately, a Greek traitor showed the Persians a secret path around the mountains, allowing them to surround the Greeks. Realizing they could not win, Leonidas and his men fought to the end, choosing to die rather than surrender. The Spartans' bravery inspired other Greek city-states to unite against the Persians, and their story has been told for thousands of years as a symbol of courage and sacrifice.

Another famous last stand took place in 1879 at the Battle of Rorke's Drift in South Africa. During the Anglo-Zulu War, a small British garrison of around 150 soldiers, many of them sick or injured, was stationed at a supply post in Rorke's Drift. They soon learned that a massive Zulu force of over 3,000 warriors was approaching. Outnumbered more than twenty to one, the British soldiers quickly built a defensive wall using bags of grain and biscuit boxes to protect themselves. The Zulus attacked repeatedly, charging the British lines with fierce determination. Despite the overwhelming odds, the British held their ground, using their rifles and discipline to repel wave after wave of attackers. The battle lasted for several hours, with the defenders running low on ammunition and energy. But each time the Zulus charged, the British soldiers held their line. By the end of the battle, the Zulus had lost many warriors, and they finally retreated, leaving the British with an unexpected victory. The courage shown by the defenders of Rorke's Drift earned them many honors and awards, and their stand became a celebrated example of bravery and resilience.

In American history, the Battle of the Alamo in 1836 is one of the most well-known last stands. At the time, Texas was fighting for independence from Mexico, and a small group of Texan and American fighters gathered at an old mission called the Alamo in San Antonio. The Mexican army, led by General Santa Anna, greatly outnumbered the defenders, bringing thousands of soldiers to attack the Alamo, which was defended by fewer than 200 men. The Texans, including famous figures like Davy Crockett, Jim Bowie, and William Travis, knew they were outnumbered, but they believed in their cause and were determined to defend their position. For 13 days, they resisted the Mexican attacks, but eventually, Santa Anna's forces broke through the walls. The defenders fought fiercely until the end, but almost all of them were killed. Though the Alamo was lost, the bravery of its defenders inspired Texans to continue fighting. The cry "Remember the Alamo!" became a rallying call, and eventually, Texas won its independence from Mexico. The Alamo stands as a symbol of courage, sacrifice, and the determination to fight for freedom.

The story of the 300 Spartans at Thermopylae isn't the only last stand from ancient times. Another famous last stand happened at the Battle of Masada around 73 CE, during the First Jewish-Roman War. Masada was a fortress built on a high plateau in the Judean Desert, and it became a refuge for a group of Jewish rebels who were resisting Roman rule. The Romans, determined to capture the fortress, built a massive ramp up the mountainside to reach the rebels. Knowing they couldn't hold out against the Romans forever, the defenders chose to take their own lives rather than be captured and enslaved. When the Romans finally broke into the fortress, they found it empty, with almost all the defenders gone. The story of Masada became a symbol of resistance and the strong desire for freedom. In Israel, Masada is remembered as a place of heroism and the will to stand up against impossible odds, even when facing powerful enemies.

During the Indian Rebellion of 1857, a last stand took place in the city of Cawnpore (now called Kanpur), India, between British forces and Indian rebels. Indian soldiers, who were once part of the British army, rose up against British rule, and Cawnpore became one of the key sites of resistance. A small group of British soldiers, women, and children took shelter in a makeshift fortress, defending themselves against a much larger force of Indian rebels. The defenders held out for several weeks, enduring attacks, food shortages, and disease. Eventually, they surrendered, believing they would be allowed to leave safely, but they were attacked again. The tragic end of the defenders of Cawnpore left a lasting impact on British and Indian history, with both sides remembering the event as a painful but important part of their struggle for power.

A more recent example of a heroic last stand happened during World War II at the Battle of Stalingrad. While not a small group, the defenders of Stalingrad made a last stand to protect their city from

German forces. Stalingrad was a critical location for the Soviet Union, and both Hitler and Stalin knew its importance. The German army attacked fiercely, and the city turned into a battleground, with intense street-by-street fighting. Soviet soldiers, civilians, and workers resisted the German advance, turning every building into a fortress and every street into a line of defense. Despite the brutal conditions, hunger, and freezing weather, the Soviets held their ground. After months of fighting, the German army was surrounded and forced to surrender, marking a turning point in the war. The defenders of Stalingrad showed incredible resilience, turning their city into a symbol of strength and determination against overwhelming odds.

In another part of World War II, the Battle of Wake Island was a heroic last stand by a small group of U.S. Marines against the Japanese. Wake Island, a small Pacific island, became a battleground when the Japanese attacked shortly after the bombing of Pearl Harbor. The Marines stationed there were heavily outnumbered, with limited supplies and support. Despite facing a powerful Japanese force with ships, planes, and many soldiers, the Marines held out for as long as they could. They managed to repel initial attacks, even sinking a Japanese destroyer and downing several planes. However, the overwhelming Japanese forces eventually overran the island. The courage and determination of the defenders, even in the face of certain defeat, made the Battle of Wake Island one of the memorable last stands in American history.

Heroic last stands aren't just about defending territory—they are about holding onto ideals, loyalty, and the belief in something greater than oneself. These moments are remembered because they show how people can be willing to sacrifice everything for their beliefs, their friends, and their homelands. Last stands are about never giving up, even when victory seems impossible. Although the defenders in these battles often knew that they would not survive, they chose to fight anyway, showing that bravery and determination can be powerful enough to inspire generations long after the battle is over.

Each last stand in history has its own story of courage, loss, and inspiration, and these moments continue to be celebrated and remembered. They teach us that sometimes, the most important battles aren't won with victory but with the willingness to stand firm in the face of overwhelming odds. The heroism shown in these last stands lives on in the tales told about them, reminding us all of the strength of the human spirit and the bravery that lies within each of us when we choose to fight for what we believe is right.

Chapter 18: Technology in Battle

Technology in battle has changed the way wars are fought throughout history. From simple weapons like spears and shields to advanced machinery like tanks, planes, and even satellites, technology has given armies new tools to defend their lands, attack enemies, and outsmart opponents. With each new invention, armies have been able to move faster, strike harder, and communicate better, often giving one side an advantage over the other. The use of technology in battle reflects human creativity and problem-solving, as people constantly look for ways to improve how they fight and protect themselves. Understanding how technology has evolved in warfare shows us how important inventions have been in shaping history and how people have adapted to changing times by developing new ways to defend themselves or gain an edge over their opponents.

In ancient times, early humans began creating simple tools like sharp stones, spears, and clubs, which gave them better ways to hunt and protect themselves. As people learned to work with metal, they created stronger and sharper weapons, such as swords, axes, and arrowheads. The invention of the bow and arrow was a major breakthrough, as it allowed warriors to attack from a distance instead of getting close to their enemies. This development changed the way battles were fought, as armies now had to plan for attacks from farther away. Armor also became important, with soldiers wearing protective gear made from leather or metal to shield themselves from enemy weapons. The chariot, a two-wheeled vehicle pulled by horses, was another early piece of technology that helped warriors move quickly on the battlefield, allowing them to charge into enemy lines or chase down fleeing opponents. In ancient Egypt and Mesopotamia, chariots gave armies an advantage because they provided both speed and mobility, allowing warriors to strike fast and then retreat before their enemies could respond.

One of the biggest technological changes in ancient warfare was the use of siege weapons. As cities grew larger and built walls for protection, armies had to find ways to break through these defenses. The battering ram, a large wooden beam, was used to smash through gates and walls, allowing soldiers to invade fortified areas. Catapults and trebuchets were developed to hurl large stones or fireballs over walls, causing damage and spreading fear among defenders. In ancient Greece and Rome, engineers built siege towers, tall wooden structures on wheels that allowed soldiers to climb up and reach the tops of walls. These inventions made it possible for armies to attack even the strongest fortresses, changing the way battles were fought and forcing cities to improve their defenses. Engineers constantly had to come up with new ways to either protect cities or break through defenses, leading to a cycle of innovation and counter-innovation.

In the Middle Ages, knights in shining armor became a symbol of military power. Mounted on horseback and wearing heavy suits of metal armor, knights were nearly unstoppable in battle. But the invention of the longbow began to change this. The longbow, which was much larger than a regular bow, could shoot arrows with enough force to pierce through a knight's armor from a great distance. This new weapon made knights vulnerable, as they could now be taken down before they reached the enemy. The crossbow, another powerful weapon that used a bow mounted on a wooden frame, also made it easier for soldiers with little training to shoot accurately. These weapons were simpler to use than swords or spears, allowing common soldiers to stand a chance against highly trained knights. Armor also began to change as blacksmiths tried to make it stronger but lighter, allowing knights to move more freely. The need to respond to new technology kept pushing military innovations, as each side tried to find ways to counter the other's advantages.

Gunpowder marked a major turning point in the history of warfare. Invented in China and eventually spread to Europe, gunpowder allowed for the creation of firearms, such as muskets and cannons. Muskets were handheld guns that fired small metal balls, while cannons were large guns that could fire heavy cannonballs over long distances. Cannons could easily destroy castle walls, making it nearly impossible for cities to rely solely on thick walls for protection. The use of firearms changed warfare completely, as soldiers no longer needed to be strong or highly trained to be effective. With gunpowder weapons, even small armies could have a huge impact, and battles became more deadly and intense. This new technology forced armies to rethink their strategies, as they could no longer rely on close combat or physical strength alone. Muskets and cannons spread across Europe and Asia, leading to the development of new tactics and formations, such as soldiers standing in rows and firing in volleys to maximize their firepower.

The Industrial Revolution in the 18th and 19th centuries brought even more advancements in military technology. Factories made it possible to produce large numbers of weapons, allowing armies to equip more soldiers with guns, ammunition, and other supplies. Railroads allowed soldiers and supplies to move quickly over long distances, making it easier to get reinforcements and resupply troops on the front lines. Ironclad ships, which were protected by metal armor, changed naval warfare, as they were much stronger than wooden ships and could withstand cannon fire. Submarines also began to emerge, allowing navies to attack ships from below the water. The invention of the telegraph allowed commanders to communicate instantly over long distances, giving armies better control and coordination on the battlefield. These technologies made wars larger and more organized, as armies could now fight in multiple locations at once and rely on factories to keep them supplied.

World War I saw some of the most dramatic changes in military technology. Machine guns, which could fire hundreds of bullets per minute, made it almost impossible for soldiers to charge across open ground without being mowed down. Poison gas was introduced, creating a new kind of danger that could spread through trenches and cause horrific injuries. Airplanes were used in battle for the first time, allowing armies to spy on enemy positions from the sky and even drop bombs. Tanks, which were heavily armored vehicles that could cross rough terrain, were invented to break through enemy lines. The tank was slow and clumsy at first, but it gave soldiers a way to cross no-man's-land, the dangerous open area between opposing trenches. Trenches themselves became an important part of the war, as soldiers dug deep networks of trenches to protect themselves from enemy fire. This new type of warfare, called "trench warfare," led to long, grueling battles with high casualties, as each side tried to break through the other's defenses.

In World War II, technology advanced even further, with some of the most powerful weapons ever created. Fighter planes, bombers, and aircraft carriers made air power a crucial part of warfare, allowing armies to strike from the skies. Radar was invented, which could detect enemy planes and ships before they arrived, giving defenders time to prepare. Submarines became a deadly threat, especially in the Atlantic, where German U-boats targeted Allied ships carrying supplies. Tanks were improved to be faster and more powerful, and armies used them in large formations to break through enemy lines. But perhaps the most significant invention was the atomic bomb, a weapon that could cause massive destruction. The United States used two atomic bombs on the Japanese cities of Hiroshima and Nagasaki in 1945, leading to the end of the war. The power of the atomic bomb shocked the world, showing how dangerous new technology could be. It also started the nuclear arms race, as countries began developing more powerful weapons to deter each other from going to war.

Today, technology in battle continues to evolve with even more advanced tools. Drones, which are unmanned aircraft, allow soldiers to spy on enemies, deliver supplies, or even attack targets without risking human lives. Satellites orbiting the Earth provide real-time information on enemy movements, weather, and terrain, helping commanders make informed decisions. Computers and artificial intelligence (AI) are used to analyze data and predict the outcomes of battles, giving armies new insights and strategies. Cyber warfare, where hackers try to disrupt enemy communications or disable systems, is becoming a major part of modern conflicts. Robots are also being developed to help soldiers with tasks like bomb disposal or carrying heavy equipment. The use of high-tech equipment like night-vision goggles and thermal imaging allows soldiers to fight effectively even in the dark, giving them an advantage in surprise attacks.

One of the most impressive uses of technology in modern warfare is stealth technology. Stealth planes, like the B-2 bomber, are designed to avoid detection by radar, allowing them to slip into enemy territory undetected. This technology makes it harder for enemies to defend against surprise attacks from the air. Precision-guided missiles, which can be directed to hit specific targets, reduce the risk of civilian casualties and make attacks more accurate. These missiles use GPS or lasers to home in on targets, making them a powerful tool for taking out key enemy positions without risking soldiers' lives.

Technology in battle has transformed warfare from small skirmishes with simple weapons to complex operations involving thousands of troops, advanced machinery, and computerized systems. Each new invention, from the bow and arrow to the stealth bomber, has shaped the way wars are fought and won, pushing armies to adapt and find new ways to protect their nations. Technology has also made war more deadly, as new weapons are often more powerful and accurate than those before. At the same time, advancements like precision-guided missiles and better armor help protect soldiers and civilians by reducing the risks of battle. The history of technology in warfare is a reminder of how human ingenuity can create tools that help us defend ourselves, and how each invention changes the nature of war, for better or worse.

Chapter 19: Communication on the Battlefield

Communication on the battlefield has always been crucial to the success of armies, allowing soldiers, leaders, and commanders to coordinate their movements, share information, and respond to unexpected challenges. The history of battlefield communication stretches back thousands of years, showing how armies have developed and used different methods to stay connected even in the chaos of war. From simple signals and messengers to sophisticated radio systems and real-time satellite links, each advancement in communication has helped armies become faster, more organized, and more effective. Good communication can mean the difference between victory and defeat, and armies have always worked to improve how they stay in touch during battles. As battles grew larger and more complex, so did the need for reliable and quick ways to pass information, keep units organized, and ensure everyone knew the plan, even when situations changed rapidly.

In ancient times, armies relied on basic forms of communication. One of the earliest methods was the use of messengers, who would run, ride horses, or even row boats to carry messages from one place to another. Messengers had to be fast and brave, as they often traveled through dangerous areas to reach their destinations. For example, during the Battle of Marathon in ancient Greece, a messenger named Pheidippides is said to have run over 26 miles to bring news of the Greek victory over the Persians back to Athens. The distance he ran is the reason we have marathons today! Messengers were often trusted individuals because the safety and accuracy of the message depended on them. If a messenger was captured or killed, the information could be lost or fall into enemy hands, which could change the outcome of a battle.

Along with messengers, ancient armies used visual signals to communicate. In Greece and Rome, soldiers used flags, torches, and smoke signals to send simple messages across distances. For example, a red flag might signal an attack, while a white flag could mean a retreat. Fire and smoke signals were often used for long distances because they could be seen from far away. In China, the Great Wall was equipped with watchtowers where soldiers would light fires to warn of approaching enemies, passing the signal along from one tower to the next so that the message could travel quickly across miles. However, these signals were limited because they could only send basic information. Armies needed to be creative in finding ways to use these signals to mean different things depending on the situation. If the weather was poor or there was fog, smoke signals could be hard to see, making communication difficult. Despite these challenges, visual signals remained an important part of communication for centuries.

The invention of the drum and bugle allowed armies to communicate orders through sound. Drums and bugles were loud enough to be heard over the noise of battle, and they could send commands like "advance," "retreat," or "charge" to groups of soldiers. Each army developed its own system of drum beats and bugle calls, allowing soldiers to understand commands without needing to see their commanders or hear words. For example, in the American Civil War, different bugle calls were used to signal when troops should wake up, go to bed, eat, or prepare for battle. Drums were especially important in medieval and early modern armies, as they were used to set the marching pace for large groups of soldiers, helping them stay in formation. The steady beat of the drum gave soldiers something to focus on, keeping their spirits high and helping them move together as one unit.

With the rise of large-scale battles in the 17th and 18th centuries, military communication became more organized. Armies began using flags and semaphore systems to send more detailed messages across longer distances. Semaphore involved signaling with hand-held flags in specific positions to represent different letters or phrases. A soldier holding two flags in certain positions could "spell out" messages letter by letter. Semaphore allowed for more complex messages than simple flag waving, but it required training, as both the sender and receiver needed to understand the signals. In the 18th and 19th centuries, the British Navy used semaphore to communicate between ships in a fleet. The system was useful because it didn't rely on sound, which could be drowned out by wind and waves, and it allowed ships to communicate even when they were too far apart to shout.

The invention of the telegraph in the 19th century revolutionized battlefield communication. The telegraph allowed messages to be sent as electrical signals over wires, sometimes spanning hundreds of miles. Using Morse code—a system of dots and dashes to represent letters—telegraph operators could send messages much faster than any messenger or flag signal. During the American Civil War, the Union Army used the telegraph to coordinate its forces over long distances. Telegraph lines were often laid along railroad tracks, allowing commanders to quickly send orders and receive updates from different parts of the battlefield. Telegraphs allowed generals to adjust their strategies based on real-time information, giving them a huge advantage. However, telegraph lines could be cut by enemy forces, so armies had to protect them to keep communication lines open.

Radio technology, developed in the early 20th century, was another major breakthrough in battlefield communication. Radios allowed soldiers to communicate without wires, making it possible to send messages from moving vehicles, ships, or airplanes. During World War I, radios were first used on a large scale, especially in naval battles where ships needed to stay in touch over vast ocean distances. Radios had the advantage of being faster and more reliable than messengers or flags, as they allowed commanders to speak directly to each other even if they were miles apart. In World War II, radio communication became even more essential, with soldiers using portable radios to stay in contact with their units. This helped them coordinate their movements, call for backup, and respond to changing situations on the ground. Radios allowed commanders to communicate with multiple units at once, making it easier to control large-scale operations and respond to enemy attacks quickly.

The development of encrypted communication was also a big part of battlefield communication during World War II. Encryption involves encoding messages so that only the intended recipient can understand them. This was important because if enemy forces intercepted radio messages, they could learn about plans and strategies. The Germans used a complex machine called the Enigma to encode their messages, but Allied codebreakers, including famous mathematician Alan Turing, eventually figured out how to crack the code. This breakthrough allowed the Allies to intercept and understand German plans, which helped them win several important battles. Encryption became a major focus in military communication, as armies looked for new ways to protect their messages and keep them secret from the enemy.

In modern times, communication on the battlefield has become even more advanced with the use of satellites, computers, and digital networks. Satellites orbiting the Earth allow armies to communicate over vast distances instantly, providing a bird's-eye view of battlefields and enemy movements. Commanders can see real-time images from drones and satellites, giving them a much better understanding of what's happening on the ground. Computers and GPS technology help soldiers navigate and find precise locations, which is important for directing airstrikes, sending reinforcements, or moving supplies to where they are needed most. Today, soldiers can carry compact communication devices that link them directly to their commanders, who can track their location, receive updates, and give orders in real time. This technology allows armies to respond to changes on the battlefield almost instantly, making them faster and more adaptable than ever before.

Drones have added a new dimension to battlefield communication, as they can fly over enemy positions to gather information without putting soldiers at risk. Drones can send live video feeds back to commanders, allowing them to see the enemy's position, movement, and defenses. This real-time information can be shared with all units, helping them make better decisions and coordinate their attacks more effectively. Drones can also be used to relay communication signals, extending the range of radios and ensuring that soldiers in remote areas stay connected. Some drones are even capable of dropping supplies to troops in hard-to-reach areas, showing how technology has made it possible to support soldiers more effectively on the battlefield.

Cyber communication and electronic warfare have become important parts of modern military strategy. Cyber warfare involves using computers and networks to disrupt an enemy's communication systems, gather intelligence, or spread misinformation. By hacking into enemy systems, armies can disable communication lines, jam signals, or even take control of enemy equipment. Cyber warfare allows armies to weaken their opponents without firing a single shot. Electronic warfare is similar, as it involves disrupting enemy signals and radar to make it harder for them to communicate or detect incoming attacks. These methods can create confusion and disrupt enemy plans, giving armies a hidden advantage. However, cyber warfare requires highly skilled experts who understand how to operate and defend complex computer systems, making it a specialized area of modern warfare.

Even with all the high-tech advancements, some traditional methods of communication, like hand signals and flares, are still used on the battlefield. In situations where radios or digital systems might not work, such as in mountainous terrain or during electronic interference, soldiers still rely on visual signals to communicate simple commands. Hand signals are quiet and quick, allowing soldiers to move and give orders without alerting the enemy. Flares can be used to signal positions, mark targets, or call for help, and are especially useful at night or in poor weather when other forms of communication might fail.

Communication on the battlefield is more than just passing along orders—it's about sharing information, coordinating movements, and responding to unexpected changes. Each new technology, from the ancient smoke signal to the latest satellite link, has brought armies closer together, making them more organized and effective. At the same time, these advancements remind us of the challenges and risks that come with war, as each side seeks to gain an advantage over the other. Good communication is essential not only for achieving victory but also for protecting lives, as it allows commanders to react quickly to danger and make better decisions for the safety of their troops. Understanding the history of battlefield communication gives us insight into how technology has shaped warfare and reminds us of the value of staying connected, especially when it matters most.

Chapter 20: Courage and Leadership

Courage and leadership are two of the most important qualities on the battlefield. These traits are what help armies achieve victory even in the toughest, most dangerous situations. Leaders with courage inspire their troops, give them confidence, and help them overcome fear, which is natural in the face of danger. Throughout history, battles have been won because leaders and soldiers showed incredible bravery and led their people with strength and wisdom. Courage is not just about being fearless—it's about doing what needs to be done even when fear is present. Leadership is about guiding others, making hard decisions, and looking out for the well-being of everyone. Together, courage and leadership can make a huge difference on the battlefield, uniting soldiers and helping them achieve goals that might seem impossible.

In ancient times, leaders often led their armies from the front, standing alongside their soldiers and facing the same dangers. For instance, Alexander the Great, one of history's most famous leaders, would charge into battle with his troops, showing them that he was willing to risk his life just like they were. His courage made his soldiers respect him deeply, and they followed him loyally across vast territories as he built an empire. Alexander's leadership was not only about fighting; he also planned his battles carefully, thinking about the strengths and weaknesses of his enemies. His courage inspired his soldiers to keep pushing forward, even when the challenges were great, because they knew he was facing the same risks.

Courage often means staying calm under pressure, something that is very important in chaotic battle situations. Julius Caesar, a Roman general, was known for his ability to stay calm and make quick decisions, even when surrounded by enemies. Once, when his army was outnumbered in Gaul, Caesar showed incredible bravery by keeping his soldiers steady, reminding them of their strengths, and encouraging them to fight smartly rather than panicking. His calmness in the face of danger helped his troops stay focused, and they were able to turn the tide of the battle. This kind of courage not only boosts the morale of soldiers but also helps leaders make wise decisions that can change the course of a battle. Caesar's courage and leadership made his army one of the most successful in ancient Rome, as they trusted him to guide them through any situation.

Leadership is also about making decisions that protect the lives of soldiers. A good leader is not someone who leads troops into battle recklessly; rather, a great leader thinks carefully about every decision, weighing the risks and benefits. During World War II, British Prime Minister Winston Churchill became a symbol of courage and leadership. Although he wasn't fighting on the front lines, his words and actions inspired his country to stay strong and never give up, even when facing difficult odds. Churchill's speeches, like his famous line "We shall fight on the beaches," gave people hope and courage to keep going during dark times. He made people feel that they were part of something bigger and that they could win if they stayed united. His leadership showed that courage isn't only about physical bravery; it's also about having mental strength, faith, and determination to keep fighting for what is right.

For soldiers, courage can mean standing firm when the situation looks hopeless. The Spartans at the Battle of Thermopylae are an excellent example of this. Led by King Leonidas, 300 Spartan soldiers faced a massive Persian army. They knew they were outnumbered, but they held their ground, showing incredible bravery. They fought to protect their homeland, even though they knew they might not survive. Leonidas's courage as a leader made his soldiers willing to face these overwhelming odds, and their stand became a symbol of bravery for centuries. The Spartans' courage didn't just help them in that one battle—it inspired other Greek city-states to unite against the Persians. Sometimes, a leader's courage can inspire an entire nation to stand strong and defend itself, even in the face of seemingly impossible odds.

A courageous leader also knows when to change tactics or retreat if it means saving lives. During the Napoleonic Wars, Marshal Michel Ney, one of Napoleon's trusted commanders, led his troops with bravery and skill. Known as "the bravest of the brave," Ney showed courage by being at the front of his men, rallying them in the heat of battle. But he also understood the importance of strategic retreats. When the French army was in a difficult position, Ney managed to guide his soldiers to safety, making sure they could live to fight another day. His courage wasn't just in fighting but also in making tough decisions under pressure. This kind of leadership shows that courage doesn't always mean charging forward; sometimes, it means choosing the path that will protect the most people, even if it requires sacrifice.

In modern warfare, courage and leadership continue to play vital roles. During World War I, soldiers had to deal with trench warfare, a brutal and dangerous form of combat where soldiers lived in muddy, cramped trenches, facing constant shelling and attacks. Conditions were harsh, and soldiers often felt scared and exhausted. Leaders who showed courage by visiting the front lines and checking on their men made a big difference. Their presence reminded soldiers that their leaders cared about them and understood the dangers they faced. Field Marshal Douglas Haig, though controversial in his methods, visited his troops and tried to encourage them to keep going. Even though he was criticized for his strategies, his willingness to be with his soldiers and lead from the front showed a kind of courage that soldiers respected.

Leadership also involves the courage to make hard decisions, even when those decisions are unpopular. During the American Civil War, President Abraham Lincoln faced the challenge of leading a nation torn apart. His decision to issue the Emancipation Proclamation was a courageous one, as it aimed to end slavery and change the purpose of the war. Lincoln knew this decision might not be accepted by everyone, but he believed it was the right thing to do. His leadership inspired many soldiers to fight not just for the Union but also for freedom and equality. This decision gave the soldiers a cause they could believe in, strengthening their resolve. Lincoln's courage in leading the country through such a difficult time showed that true leadership is not about pleasing everyone; it's about doing what you believe is right.

Sometimes, leaders show courage by putting the needs of others before their own. In World War II, Lieutenant Audie Murphy became one of the most decorated American soldiers by risking his life multiple times to protect his fellow soldiers. On one occasion, he single-handedly held off an entire German company, allowing his unit to escape to safety. His courage and selflessness saved many lives, and his actions became legendary. Murphy's leadership was based on his willingness to do whatever it took to protect those around him, even if it put him in great danger. This kind of courage reminds us that a true leader is someone who cares deeply about the people they lead and is willing to put others before themselves.

Courage is not limited to soldiers and generals; sometimes, ordinary people show incredible bravery on the battlefield. During World War II, people in occupied countries risked their lives to help soldiers and resist enemy forces. Members of the French Resistance, for example, worked secretly to sabotage the German army and gather information for the Allies. These brave men and women showed courage by standing up to a powerful enemy, even though they knew they could be captured or worse. Their leadership came from a strong belief in freedom and the courage to act on it, proving that courage is not only about physical strength but also about mental strength and a commitment to what is right.

Leadership and courage can also be seen in moments of peace, when soldiers and leaders work to rebuild and help others after the fighting is over. After wars end, leaders must have the courage to make difficult decisions about rebuilding and reconciliation. After World War II, General Douglas MacArthur helped lead the rebuilding efforts in Japan. He worked to establish democratic reforms and helped Japan recover from the devastation of war. This kind of leadership required patience, vision, and the courage to build bridges between former enemies. MacArthur's efforts helped Japan become one of America's closest allies, showing that courage and leadership can heal as well as protect.

In more recent history, stories of courage and leadership continue to inspire people. For example, during the Gulf War, General Norman Schwarzkopf led the coalition forces with a strong sense of purpose and determination. Known for his straightforward approach and dedication to his troops, Schwarzkopf earned the respect of soldiers and leaders alike. He took time to explain his strategies to his soldiers, making sure they understood the reasons behind his decisions. This transparency and commitment helped build trust and loyalty among his troops, and they followed his lead with confidence. Schwarzkopf's leadership demonstrated that courage also means being open and honest with those you lead, showing that you are in it together.

Leadership on the battlefield also involves taking responsibility for one's actions. A good leader does not blame others when things go wrong; instead, they take responsibility and work to fix the problem. This courage to accept responsibility builds trust and shows soldiers that their leader cares about doing the right thing. Leaders who show courage and take responsibility for their decisions earn the loyalty and respect of their troops, creating a strong, united team.

Courage and leadership go hand in hand. A courageous leader inspires others, gives them strength, and helps them believe in themselves. Whether they are facing physical dangers on the battlefield or making difficult decisions in a time of crisis, leaders who show courage have the power to bring out the best in others. From ancient heroes to modern generals, the history of courage and leadership on the battlefield shows us that bravery is not just about fighting—it's about leading by example, caring for others, and standing up for what you believe in. True leaders are not only brave in battle but also have the courage to do what is right, even when it is difficult. They inspire others to overcome their fears, follow their lead, and work together to achieve goals that no one could accomplish alone.

Epilogue

Now that you've explored the incredible strategies and clever tactics that have shaped battles throughout history, you've seen how much more there is to warfare than just strength and numbers. Behind every victory and every daring escape lies the power of a well-thought-out plan, patience, and sometimes, the courage to do the unexpected. These strategies weren't only about winning a battle—they changed the course of history, shaping countries, empires, and even the world we know today.

The people who created these strategies didn't always have the best weapons or the largest armies, but they knew how to use their resources wisely. They understood the power of nature, the importance of knowing their enemies, and the impact of working together. Many of these ideas have inspired not only soldiers but also leaders in every field, from explorers to inventors, showing that smart thinking can solve even the toughest problems.

As you close this book, remember that strategy isn't just about war. It's a tool you can use in everyday life—to solve problems, make plans, and think ahead. The greatest minds of history remind us that patience, creativity, and courage are often the keys to success.

So, whether you're facing a big challenge or making a decision, think like a strategist. Who knows? Maybe one day, you'll create a game-changing plan of your own. The art of strategy isn't just history—it's a way of thinking that will always have the power to change the world.

The End.